BABES IN THE WOOD

A PANTOMIME

JIM SPERINCK

Jasper Publishing
1 Broad St Hemel Hempstead Herts HP2 5BW
Tel; 01442 63461 Fax; 01442 217102

To obtain information about acting fees payable on all professional and amateur performances of this play, together with any other details, please apply to the publishers;

Jasper Publishing

1 Broad Street Hemel Hempstead
Herts HP2 5BW
Tel; 01442 63461 Fax; 01442 217102

A licence must first be obtained before any performance can be given, and fees are payable in advance.

British Library Cataloguing-in-Publication Data
A catalogue record for this book is available from the British Library

ISBN 1 874009 35 X

CHARACTERS

Tom	] the
Mary	] Babes
Baron Stoneyheart	Sheriff of Nottingham
Nickle	] Sheriff's
Dime	] henchmen
Sunny Spells	Fairy Queen
Firefly	Assistant Fairy Queen
Maid Marion	in love with Robin Hood
Nurse Nightingale	nurse to the Babes
Robin Hood	
Little John	] Robin's
Friar Tuck	] band
Will Scarlet	] of
Tom Farrier	] Merry
Much the Miller	] Men
Desmond the Deer	

General Chorus as: servants, maids, soldiers and guards of the Castle, villagers, foresters, Merry Men, junior fairies, school children, toys, animals and forest creatures etc.,

SYNOPSIS OF SCENES

ACT 1

Scene 1	Inside the Castle at Nottingham
Scene 2	Somewhere in the Castle grounds
Scene 3	The Castle Schoolroom
Scene 4	Nurse Nightingale's Bedroom

ACT 2

Scene 1	In Sherwood Forest
Scene 2	Robin Hood's Camp
Scene 3	A Dungeon in the Castle
Scene 4	The Reception Hall of the Castle

Scenery may be kept very simple if desired. Alternatively, this pantomime offers the opportunity to put on a really lavish production - the choice is yours. There is a short, interact scene, between each of the main scenes that will allow sufficient time for big scene changes. These interact scenes can easily be played in front of tabs, or, if facilities allow, a front cloth.

Most principals can wear the same costume throughout the show, with the possible exception of the finale scene. Please refer to the Production Notes at the end of the script.

NOTES ON THE CHARACTERS

Tom and Mary. The 'Babes' of the story. They can be almost any age up to say 12ish. The number of lines has been limited here to enable quite small children to be used. They need to appear vulnerable, but they stand up to the Sheriff, and have a child's natural suspicion of him.

Sheriff Stoneyheart. Traditional pantomime villian who relishes his badness, and struts arrogantly about the stage, as he is booed by the audience. He wants to marry Maid Marion, and dispose of the Babes to inherit his brother's, much needed money. Male.

Nickle. The smarter of the two henchmen, and clearly in charge. These two go along with the Sheriff, rather than actively support him, and they eventually desert him at the end. Male.

Dime. The dumb, but more loveable, half of the henchmen duo. He will have the audience on his side, as he bears the brunt of jokes from Sheriff and Nickle. He trusts Nickle, and goes along with him. Must be able to relate to the audience, and strike up a rapport with them. Male.

Sunny Spells. Not quite a traditional Fairy Queen, who gets off to a slow start, but, encouraged by Firefly, and the audience, sorts the Sheriff out, most aptly, at the end. Female.

Firefly. Assistant Fairy Queen, who needs all her dedication to motivate Sunny Spells, with some comedy resulting for the 'fairy duo'. Female.

Maid Marion. Principal girl. Should be a clear contrast in years to the Babes, and needs to be played by a mature actress, who can command the stage. She is protective towards the Babes, suspicious of the Sheriff, practical, dependable, with an established relationship with Robin Hood. Female.

Nurse Nightingale. In many ways the traditional pantomime dame. Feather-brained, man-crazy, likes her drink, and game for anything. Needs plenty of energy, versatility, quick changes of mood, and command of the stage. Male.

Robin Hood. Principal boy. Keen to help Maid Marion in her quest to save the Babes. Needs to look right with Maid Marion, and to command his Merry Men. Female.

Merry Men. Can be played by an all male, all female, or mixed group. More (or even less) members could be added, if desired, with the lines re-allocated.

Desmond the Deer. He could easily become 'Harold the Horse'. He would then have been 'illtreated' by the Sheriff, not shot, with the 'venison' joke cut.

MUSICAL NUMBERS

The songs included here are <u>suggestions only</u> for the type of music that can be used. Final choice is left to the Musical Director.

Please note that permission from **Jasper Publishing** to perform this play **does** **not** include permission to use copyright songs and music suggested here. Performers are urged to consult the **Performing Right Society** (see note below).

Overture - English country music, or theme music

1.	Opening number, "It's Gonna Be A Great Day" or another	Full chorus
2.	Duet, "I Have Dreamed" or "Love Me, That's All I Ask Of You" or another	Marion and Robin
3.	"Money, Money, Money" or "Money Makes The World Go Around"	Sheriff
4.	"You've Got To Pick A Pocket Or Two" adapted, or another	Nickle and Dime
5.	"Fortuosity" or another	Nurse, Marion, and chorus
6.	Ballet or Pop Music	Junior chorus dance
7.	"Three Little Maids From School"	Sheriff, Nickle, Dime
8.	"March Of The Toys" or another	Junior chorus dance
9.	"The Stripper"	Background only
10.	"Robin Hood, Robin Hood"	House Song. Nickle, Dime and Sheriff
11.	Dance to Ballet Music	Forest creatures

12.	"I Love Those Lazy, Hazy Days Of Summer" or "Busy Doin' Nothing" or "Gone Fishing"	Merry Men and chorus
13.	"How You Gonna Keep Him Down On The Farm" adapted, or "Tit Willow" or "Old MacDonald Had A Farm"	Much and Nurse Nightingale
14.	Reprise, Music No 12, or another	Merry Men
15.	Reprise, Music No 2, or "This Nearly Was Mine" or "Somewhere"	Marion and Robin
16.	"On A Wonderful Day Like Today" or "If I Were A Bell"	Full chorus
17.	Heroic March	Background only
18.	"Get Me To The Church" adapted	Sheriff and Nurse
19.	"On A Wonderful Day Like Today" or any up-tempo number from show	Full Chorus

*The following statement (provided by the **Performing Right Society Ltd.,**) concerning the use of music, is included here for your attention.*

The permission of the owner of the performing right in copyright music must be obtained before any public performance may be given, whether in conjunction with a play or sketch or otherwise, and this permission is just as necessary for amateur performances as for professional. The majority of copyright musical works (other than oratorios, musical plays and similar dramatico-musical works) are controlled in the British Commonwealth by the **Performing Right Society Ltd., 29-33 Berners Street, London W1P 4AA.**

The Society's practice is to issue licences authorising the use of its repertoire to the proprietors of premises at which music is publicly performed, or, alternatively, to the organisers of musical entertainment, but the Society does not require payment of fees by performers as such. Producers or promoters of plays, sketches etc., at which music is to be performed, during or after the play or sketch, should ascertain whether the premises at which the performances are to be given are covered by a licence issued by the Society, and if they are not, should make application to the Society for particulars as to the fee payable.

For

Weaam and **Fahad**

BABES IN THE WOOD

ACT 1

After the overture, a dramatic chord, curtain rises and opening number begins

Scene 1

Grand Reception Hall of Nottingham Castle. Backcloth to show walls with; stained windows, armour, shields, flags, heraldic banners, arches etc., Perhaps a grand staircase. Wings to provide arched entrances etc.,

Full chorus of; castle maids, servants, guards and soldiers, villagers, Robin Hood and his men, Maid Marion, Nickle and Dime etc., all are gathered to sing and dance the opening number, 'It's Gonna be a Great Day' or another

Song No. 1

After the song Nickle and Dime exit, and some of the junior chorus may exit also. Maid Marion steps forward

Maid Marion Hello everyone, I'm Maid Marion ...

Chorus cheer

...and I live in this big castle - with my uncle - the Sheriff of Nottingham.

Chorus boo

...and this is my boy-friend Robin Hood.

Chorus cheer as Robin Hood steps forward to join Maid Marion

Robin Hood (*to audience*) Hello everyone. (*to Marion*) Marion, when, oh when, are we going to get married?
Maid Marion Soon I hope Robin. As soon as I can get my uncle's consent.
Robin Hood Old Nottingham Nasty, he'll never consent, the miserable ...

Maid Marion (*stopping him*) Robin, no bad language in front of the nice people.

Robin Hood Anyway, he wants to marry you himself.

Maid Marion (*embarrassed, and changing the subject quickly*) Yes, well, er, Robin - have you brought Desmond with you today?

Robin Hood Yes, he's outside.

Maid Marion Do you think these people would like to see Desmond?

Robin Hood Let's ask them, shall we?

Maid Marion (*to audience*) Would you like to see lovely, cuddly Desmond?

Audience Yes.

Maid Marion (*to Robin*) They don't sound very sure, do they?

Robin Hood No. Let's ask them again.

Maid Marion Would you like to see lovely, lovable cuddly Desmond?

Audience Yes.

Maid Marion points to one side of the stage, and everyone looks in that direction, then, to a drum roll, Dime walks on from the other side

Dime Here I am then!

Maid Marion Oh not you Dime. They want to see Desmond.

Dime Oh.

Marion and Robin call Desmond. Then encourage audience to call. A spot on the wings, Desmond the Deer (or Harold the Horse, see production notes) enters. Coming forward, the chorus crowd round him

Chorus Ah!

Maid Marion Hello Desmond.

Desmond nods

Maid Marion Say hello to the children.

Desmond nods to the audience

Desmond had a bad accident. The Sheriff shot you with an arrow, didn't he?

Desmond nods, turns to show other side, with large plaster patch on his rump

Chorus Ah!

Maid Marion Robin rescued you, didn't he? And now you're getting better.

Desmond nods again

You've been very brave, haven't you? But you don't like the Sheriff any more.

Desmond shakes his head

You like Robin though. He's your friend, isn't he?

Desmond nods

Robin Hood Right Men. Take him and find him something to eat.
Merry Men Right Robin etc.,
Robin Hood (*as they exit*) Say goodbye to the children.

Desmond lifts front leg and waves. Then exits, with Dime and the rest of the chorus, leaving Maid Marion and Robin Hood alone on stage

Robin Hood You changed the subject very craftily, just then, when we were talking about getting married.
Maid Marion (*rather guilty*) Yes Robin.
Robin Hood (*teasing*) Perhaps you've changed your mind. Perhaps you don't want to get married any more.
Maid Marion (*getting her own back*) Well, there is Kevin Costner to think about. He may make me an offer I can't refuse!
Robin Hood Kevin Costner? Never heard of him!
Maid Marion On the other hand, perhaps I will just settle for you.
Robin Hood That's more like it.

Song No 2

Robin and Marion sing, 'I have Dreamed' or 'Love Me' or another.

At the end of the song, one of the chorus returns running

Chorus 1 Watch out everyone, the Sheriff is on his way back. (*exits*)
Maid Marion Robin! Go quickly. The Sheriff mustn't find you here.
Robin Hood (*hesitating*) But I don't want to go!
Maid Marion Robin! Go! Please! (*pushes him off*)

Robin Hood exits, leaving Maid Marion alone on stage. Enter the Sheriff, carrying suitcase marked 'Sea Link' or 'Happy Coach Tours' or whatever

Sheriff I'm back! Put the kettle on. I hope that wasn't merriment, and people singing that I could hear, just then. Everything's been kept quiet and miserable, how I like it, while I've been away, Maid Marion?

Maid Marion (*with a smile*) Oh yes, it's been very quiet.

Sheriff Good. I hope the village riff-raff haven't been taking liberties with me ancestral dwelling ?

Maid Marion (*all innocence*) Of course not. Did you have a good time then?

Sheriff Good? Huh! I arrived in Benidorm two weeks before the hotel!

Maid Marion Oh!

Sheriff Pity you chose not to come with me Marion. I invited you, but you refused. Can't think why. A free holiday to (*local town*) is not to be sniffed at.

Maid Marion No uncle.

Sheriff (*coming close to Marion*) Now Marion, me dear, have you given any thought to that little matter we were discussing?

Maid Marion (*moving away*) Er, no uncle.

Sheriff (*growing impatient*) Well you'd better make up your mind soon. Dash it all, a fellow can't be patient forever!

Maid Marion You've been very kind to me. But I can only marry for love.

Sheriff Love! A load of rubbish! You've been watching Neighbours again, haven't you ?

Maid Marion (*changing subject, producing two letters, giving one to Sheriff*) Letters came for you while you were away. One's marked urgent.

Sheriff (*snatching the letter*) Letter, why didn't you say so. Perhaps I've won the pools. (*opens letter and reads*) What's this? Double glazing? We will be in your area for the next two weeks and would like to call...

Maid Marion No not that one. (*they exchange letters*) This one.

Sheriff (*reading the second letter*) Oh no!

Maid Marion Not bad news?

Sheriff Course it's bad news. What other news is there? Me brother, Methuselah, he's passed on, and his two brats are coming here to be looked after.

Maid Marion How much money did he leave?

Sheriff All of it. You have to. More mouths to feed. Might as well change me name to Barnados! Fetch Nickle and Dime, I want a word with them.

Maid Marion Yes uncle. (*exits*)

Sheriff (*changing mood quickly*) Little does she know, me plan is falling into place nicely. As soon as I've married Maid Marion, and killed these two kids, all the family money will be in mine. Just think, cordless phones in every room! Answer phones in the cells - BT will make even more profit! Virtual Reality games in the torture chambers! It's a good job they don't know how broke I really am. I need money. I've asked for it, begged for it, cheated for it.

Chorus (*from the wings*) Why don't you work for it?

Sheriff Because I'm going through the alphabet, and I haven't come to W yet. Streuth! I hope I never will. Oh yes, I'm as broke as the Ten Commandments. Here goes then folks - Kenneth Clarke's Lament.

Song No 3

Solo, 'Money, Money, Money,' or 'Money Makes the World go Around'

At the end of the song

Sheriff Where are those two layabouts? (*exits, shouting*) Nickle, Dime?

White spot on the wings and enter, to a tinkling of bells, Fairy Queen, Sunny Spells, pushed on stage by her assistant, Firefly

Firefly Come on Fairy Queen. You're needed. (*indicating audience*) I bet these people were beginning to wonder whether there was a Fairy Queen in this pantomime. You're supposed to come on at the beginning and do your prologue bit. You know, explaining the plot, and telling them that everything is going to be alright. What happened to that?

Sunny Spells I was watching Keith Floyd on the telly.

Firefly What was he cooking?

Sunny Spells Fairy cakes.

Firefly I shouldn't have asked! (*to the audience*) She's not been herself lately. Come on, Fairy Queen. You're not going to let the Sheriff kill the Babes are you? You must prevent it.

Sunny Spells I'm putting in for early retirement. Hang up my Fairy wand, travel a bit, and catch up on some gardening.

Firefly WHAT! You can't let all these people down! They're relying on you.

Sunny Spells You don't realise - being perfectly good all the time has distinct disadvantages.

Firefly (*very innocent*) Has it?

Sunny Spells You'll understand - when you're older.

Firefly You used to speak in rhyme once. What happened to that?

Sunny Spells It's gone out of fashion. My skills are redundant really.

Firefly Don't say that. (*to audience*) You want a Fairy Queen, don't you?

Audience Yes.

Firefly Louder. You want a Fairy Queen, don't you?

Audience YES!

Firefly Say, 'Come on Fairy Queen, get cracking'.

Audience Come on Fairy Queen, get cracking!

Firefly Now, whenever you see the Fairy Queen come on, shout out, 'Come on Fairy Queen, get cracking'. That'll encourage her. Will you do that?

Audience Yes!

Firefly Good! One more practise. Really loud. Come on Fairy Queen, get cracking.

Audience Come on Fairy Queen, get cracking!

Firefly Great! We'll have her back to normal in no time. (*to Fairy Queen*) Try to say something in rhyme now, go on, just for me.

Sunny Spells (*herself again*) Oh, alright then, if I must. We'll save the little Babes, or bust!

Firefly Great! Great! Come on, we'd better work out a plan.

Sunny Spells Surely you mean, 'Tis time for us to make a plan. And save the children, if we can.

Firefly That's better. (*to audience*) She's back to normal, alright.

They both exit one side, Fairy Queen first

Firefly (*as she exits, to the audience*) Don't forget now - when you see her again - 'Come on Fairy Queen, get cracking'.

Enter the Sheriff, from the other side, with Nickle and Dime

Sheriff (*sees Fairy duo exit*) Who's that? (*sniffs*) There's a nasty smell of goodness round here. Hope it's not catching. I must get one of those air-un-fresheners.

Nickle You wanted to see us boss?

Sheriff Yes. About time you did something for your living. I've got a little job for you. Or should I say, ha, ha, two little jobs.

Nickle Yes boss.

Sheriff Right now, listen carefully. I shall say this only once. Tomorrow two little orphans are coming to stay with me.

Dime Oh, that's nice. Can we play with them boss?

Sheriff Streuth! Listen will you? They'll be travelling through the forest, and I want you to go and meet them.

Dime Oh great! We can have a picnic.

Sheriff Picnic! This is going to be no picnic. You're to slit their throats, and bury them in the forest.

Dime (*looks round at scenery*) Crikey! I thought this was a pantomime, not an 'orror movie!

Nickle What did they do boss?

Sheriff Do? They didn't do nothing. And they're not going to get a chance. They inherit all the family money, if I don't get rid of them.

Dime Oh. Who inherits it, if you do get rid of them?

Nickle (*to Sheriff*) Huh, really thick ain't he boss?

Sheriff Yea, the lights are on, but no-one's at home.

Nickle (*to Dime, pointing to Sheriff*) He inherits, nitwit.

Dime Oh - Nitwit does. Who's he then?

Sheriff (*to audience*) Nickle and Dime, the two-bit crooks! And I was hoping to get past this scene tonight! Listen, I'm supposed to be explaining the plot to these people, not answering your stupid questions.

Nickle It's not the questions that are stupid boss, it's him.

Sheriff Look, me elder brother has shuffled off his cooking foil, er, mortal toil, er, well, anyway, his will says that I inherit everything - if anything nasty happens to his little horrors - I mean - darlings.

Dime Ah, we'll see nothing happens to them boss.

Sheriff Streuth and double streuth! I asked the producer to get me Al Capone, and I end up with these two! Look stupid...

Dime Oh, OK boss (*he pulls faces, goes cross-eyed etc*)

Sheriff What's he doing now?

Nickle (*to Dime*) What you doing?

Dime (*pulls face*) He said 'look stupid' so that's what I'm trying to do.

Nickle Huh, you don't need to practise doing that.

Sheriff Will you listen to me! There's just one condition in the will, you see, before I can get me hands on the lovely lolly loot.

Nickle What's that boss?

Sheriff I've got to be married, to inherit all the money.

Dime Ah. But you're not married, are you?

Sheriff I will be when I get Maid Marion to say yes.

Dime But she's not going to say yes. She fancies that Robin Hood.

Sheriff He's a right little ray of sunshine, isn't he? I'm going to have to fix Robin Hood as well. That's another little job for you.

Nickle Going to be busy aren't we? Will we get a bonus for overtime?

Dime We don't want to go to the forest Nick, that's where he lives, Robin Hood. He's a d-d-dangerous outlaw, and he shoots people with arrows and things, and he's got a great big g-g-gang of robbers with him.

Sheriff Is he naturally stupid, or does he practice a lot? Will you do what you're told! Off to the forest and wait for the Babes.

Enter Maid Marion, who stands behind them and looks over their shoulders, as they huddle together like a bunch of conspirators

...They'll be travelling with a nurse. When you find them (*he draws finger across throat to finish the sentence*)

*Nickle and Dime both draw fingers over their throats, conspiratorially, as Maid
Marion looks from one to the other*

Nickle You can rely on us boss, nothing frightens us.
Maid Marion (*speaking behind them, looking curiously at signs, and touching
her own throat*) UNCLE, I've made up the beds in the nursery for the Babes.

Sheriff, Nickle and Dime all jump when she speaks

Nickle OH! ER!
Dime Beds? Oh, but we won't be needing them now, will we?
Sheriff Streuth! Will you shut up you fool!
Dime (*to Nickle*) He's talking to you.
Sheriff (*to Marion*) Thank you my dear. Very thoughtful of you. (*to Nickle and
Dime*) Off you go then.
Dime Where to boss?
Sheriff To the forest. (*drawing fingers across throat, trying not to let Marion see*)
Dime Oh, to the forest. What for boss?
Sheriff Get him out of here before I slit <u>his</u> throat!
Nickle Come on. Get going. *(exits)*
Dime (*skipping round the stage as he exits*) Are we going to pick bluebells?
Maid Marion (*repeating fingers across throat sign*) What's all this mean then?
Sheriff Oh, er, I was just, er, telling him he needed a haircut. Yes, that's it.
Maid Marion (*puzzled*) Oh. Funny place for a haircut.
Sheriff They're supposed to be funny dear, they're the comedians.
Maid Marion Won't it be nice to have happy little smiling faces round the castle?
Sheriff Yes, my face will be smiling alright - soon.
Maid Marion Of course, they will cheer you up no end.
Sheriff Yes, they'll cheer me up, (*doing slit throat action to the audience*) as soon
as they've done the job.
Maid Marion Oh they won't let you down, they'll be as good as gold. Playing
round the castle with their little toys.
Sheriff Yes. (*puzzled*) Ey? Toys? I think we've got a crossed line here somewhere.
Anyway, I've got work to do. The business of the Manor must go on. I know, I'll
make a few of me peasants homeless before lunch. that'll cheer me up a bit.
Ha! Oh, 'a Sheriff's job is not an 'appy one'. Ha! Excuse me, my dear. *(exits)*
Maid Marion Hmm, there's something strange going on. (*to audience*) Did you
see this? (*repeats the fingers across the throat action*)
Audience Yes.
Maid Marion I think he's up to no good, don't you?
Audience Yes.

Maid Marion Right. I'll send someone to warn Robin Hood. Make sure the Babes get through the forest safely. *(exits)*

Nickle *(entering)* Come on Dime, we're supposed to be in the forest by now.

Enter Dime, armed to the teeth with swords, daggers, arrows, rifles, pistols, mallet, club, stave, outsize pair of scissors, crossbow etc.,

(seeing Dime's weaponry) Look at him, James Bond, licensed to kill. What do you need that lot for, we're only going to kill a couple of babies?

Dime It's for the forest Nick. In case we meet any of them robbers.

Nickle Huh, they'll be terrified of you!

Dime *(holding up rifle)* If they t-rifle with us *(holding up club)* we can club together *(holding up scissors)* cut them off at the ankles - and de-feet them. Then we make them bite the mallet.

Nickle What for?

Dime To prove they're a bunch of 'ammer-chewers. D'you get it, ammer-chewers!

Nickle I don't believe it.

Dime Then what will have happened?

Nickle They'll have died laughing, I should think.

Dime Wrong! *(holding up arrow)* We'll have had an 'arrow escape!

Nickle You won't have a narrow escape, if the Sheriff catches you.

Song No 4

A duet from Nickle and Dime. 'Carefully on Tip Toe Stealing' or 'You've got to Pick a Pocket or Two' or another

If latter song is chosen, the following words are suggested. The original words will also fit, so a combination of both new, and original, words is possible

> In this life, one thing counts,
> Doing what the Sheriff wants.
> And if it's a crime, to do this time,
> You can rely on us two, boys.
> You can rely on us two, boys.
> You can rely on us two.
> If we don't the Sheriff please,
> He's got a dungeon for two.
> If we don't the Sheriff please,
> We're in that dungeon for two!

> Why do we break our backs,
> Collecting up the Sheriff's tax?
> Ten per cent each time, goes to Nickle and Dime.
> But don't tell the Sheriff will you, boys?
> But don't tell the Sheriff will you, boys?
> But don't tell the Sheriff will you?
> We do just as we please,
> So long as the Sheriff don't know.
> We do just as we please,
> So long as the Sheriff don't know.

At the end of the song

Nickle Come on, you little Arnold Schwarzenegger you.

Nickle and Dime exit. As they exit, the Nurse, dressed for travelling, enters from the other side, watching them

Nurse I wonder who they are? Going to do some gardening, by the look of it. What a journey (*takes drink from hip flask*) that's better! Come along children.

Babes, Tom and Mary, enter, loaded down with suitcases and bags etc., They sit on the cases, exhausted

There, don't dawdle! You can have a nice rest now. I hope they won't mind us arriving early. (*looking around*) It's nice here isn't it? Just like that ..... (*local shopping arcade*) I wonder which way the wine cellar is? Very posh. I wonder if the Sheriff is married? Now you must remember your manners, and call your uncle 'Your Highness' or, if he's very short, 'Your Lowness'. And no eating peas with your knife. They never do things like that in these 'igh class 'ouses. (*takes another drink*)

They all 'freeze' as, to the tinkling of bells, the Fairy Queen enters, in a white spot, with Firefly. Firefly encourages the audience to shout

Audience Come on Fairy Queen, get cracking!
Sunny Spells Beware the Sheriff. Do not trust him.
                          His deeds are worthy of the dustbin.
Firefly (*pulling a face*) Well, it's a start, I suppose.
Sunny Spells Know that danger's lurking here.
                          But I will guard you, have no fear.

Firefly Hmm, a little rusty, but moving in the right direction.

They both exit, to a tinkling of bells. Nurse, Tom and Mary 'unfreeze'

Nurse (*holding head as though trying to remember something*) What was that? You'll find the Sheriff in the dustbin? Something about lurking here - murking - have a murky fear, beer? Strange? I must be hearing things. I need a drink to sober me up. (*takes another drink from flask*)

Tom I don't like it here. Can we go home?

Nurse Home? This is your home now.

Mary I don't like it either. It's creepy. There's something funny going on.

Nurse Well let's hope the audience thinks so.

Mary I want to go home.

Enter the Sheriff, singing 'Everything's coming up roses' happily to himself. He stops in his tracks when he sees the visitors

Sheriff What you doing invading me baronial appurtenances?

Nurse I never touched them! (*slyly to herself*) Not yet, anyway.

Sheriff Oh Gawd, you're not them are you? (*looking around for Nickle and Dime*) How did you get past me cut-throat brigade?

Nurse (*interrupting*) How nice to meet you, your Frightful-ness. These are your poor brother's orphans, (*pointing to Tom*) he's come to throw himself upon your mercy (*pointing to Mary*) she's come to throw herself upon your mercy, and I've come to throw myself upon you too.

Sheriff MERCY!

Nurse There was no-one to meet us, so we came straight in.

Sheriff Streuth! There was a reception committee waiting, but you seem to have slipped past them. I'll kill them when I catch them.

Nurse Say hello to your uncle, Tom and Mary.

Sheriff Tom and Jerry?

Nurse Tom and MARY.

Sheriff steps forward to Babes, but Tom, to a crash, kicks him on the shin

Sheriff Ouch!

Tom We want to go home!

Nurse Now Tom, behave yourself. You mustn't do things like that until you're better acquainted. (*to Sheriff*) And I am Nurse Nightingale, me first name's Synglika, do you get it?

Sheriff Synglika? That's foreign isn't it? (*pulling a face*) Oh I see, sing like a nightingale. (*not amused*) Very funny.

Nurse Well don't force yourself. You might strain something. (*getting amorous*) You can call me Nightie for short.

Tom, to a crash, kicks him again

Sheriff Ouch! (*rubbing his shin*) Nightie? Nightie for short? How short?

Nurse (*going coy*) Oh you mustn't ask a girl such intimate questions, naughty boy! (*gives him slap on the shoulders*) If you must know, it's like a good speech...

Sheriff What?

Nurse Yes, long enough to cover the subject, but short enough to be interesting! Oh, the old jokes are always the best!

Sheriff (*to audience*) That jokes even older than her, decrepit old ratbag!

Tom, to a crash, kicks him again, and this time he falls on the floor

Sheriff HELP! WILL YOU STOP DOING THAT!

Mary WE WANT TO GO HOME!

Nurse (*coming forward*) Shall I give you the kiss of life?

Sheriff (*getting up quickly*) No thanks! I feel much better already.

Nurse (*taking out hip flask and having a swig*) Well would you like a snifter - a little drop of what killed mother? (*offers him the flask*)

Sheriff NO I WOULD NOT! (*hops about on one leg rubbing shin as Babes laugh*)

Maid Marion (*entering*) Oh, how lovely, you've arrived. (*sees Sheriff hopping about*) You're playing games with them already uncle. You couldn't wait!

Sheriff Wait? I can't wait to kill the little... (*looks at Maid Marion and corrects himself*) er, thrill, what a thrill to meet the little, er, yes.

Maid Marion Come along, let uncle rest now. Plenty of time for games later. I'll show you to the nursery.

Nurse Oh I need a rest. I'm so tired from carrying those heavy cases. (*tickling the Sheriff under the chin, smiling*) See you later Uncley-Wunkley.

All exit, except the Sheriff. The Babes and Maid Marion carrying the cases

Sheriff Uncley Wunkley! Nightingale! Stupid name for a nurse! More like a vulture, if you ask me! Streuth! Me evil scheme foiled. I'll have to go over to plan B - B for <u>b</u>ashing them over the head, and <u>b</u>oiling them in oil!

Nurse (*returning*) Boiling them in oil! You must be talking about cooking some chips for the Babes' dinner. How kind! I don't know about bashing them over the head though. We usually peel ours!

Sheriff You again!

Nurse (*coming close to Sheriff and giving him the eye*) Oh, you'll make someone a wonderful husband!

Sheriff (*moving away*) Streuth! I'll have to throw a bucket of cold water over her! I think I'll give her the bird! Nightingale - the bird! Ha, ha. You still here? Was there something you wanted?

Nurse (*moving close again and hitting him*) Oh you naughty boy!

Sheriff (*moves away*) I'll re-phrase that. Are you here for any particular reason?

Nurse Oh I remember now. I shall be starting a little school here. So that the Babes can continue their education. All the local children are invited.

Sheriff Oh! Is that all?

Nurse Is that all? Who else do you want me to invite? Now, how about if I make you a nice hot cup of cocoa? I'll bring it up to your room (*slyly*) if you'll show me which one it is.

Sheriff (*exiting quickly*) Let's get out of here!

Nurse (*to audience*) Oh, one of the shy ones eh. I didn't realise there were any left in (*local town*) Still, I think he fancies me girls, don't you? Oh yes. He had that hungry look in his eyes. I can tell, you see. Oh, yes, he was smouldering alright. If I play my cards right here, I could end up Mrs. Sheriff, Lady of the Manor. Well, I've been lonely, you know, since me husband popped off. Still, I mustn't grumble, we were deliriously happy for twenty years you know, yes - until we met. And then something terrible happened to him - I married him. I didn't mind being married really, but the hours are too long. Well, I'm not cut out for all that night work you see. No. He'd have divorced me if he could have done it without making me happy. Then, one day, I sent him down to B & Q for a Black and Decker Workmate, and he never came back. No! That was six years ago - he must be served by now! He must have thought I said playmate, not workmate. Still, I can see everything's going to turn out fine now.

Nurse 'freezes' again as, to a tinkling of bells, Sunny Spells enters, in a white spot, with Firefly, who again encourages audience to shout

Audience Come on Fairy Queen, get cracking!

Sunny Spells Hear me now, or all will not be fine.
Beware the Sheriff's hideous design.
It's coming back, this knack of speaking rhyme!
(*dramatically*)
BEWARE THE SHERIFF'S HIDEOUS DESIGN!

Firefly and Sunny Spells exit, to a tinkling of bells, as Nurse 'unfreezes'

Nurse (*holds head*) There it is again! (*dramatically, imitating Fairy Queen*) Repair the Sheriff's hideous behind! Hideous behind! Well, he's not much from the front either, is he? I suppose he's torn his trousers, at the back. I'll soon mend those. I wonder who keeps saying that? (*to audience*) Who is it?
Audience The Fairy Queen!
Nurse Fairy Queen? Oh no. They don't have Fairy Queen's here. That's only in pantomimes and things.

Some of the chorus, servants, villagers etc., come on with Maid Marion

Maid Marion Nurse, some of my friends would like to meet you.
Nurse So pleased to make your h'acquaintance. I'm Nurse Nightingale.

They all exchange greetings as the rest of the chorus enter

I was telling these nice people (*nods to audience*) everything's turning out fine.
Maid Marion Yes, of course it is.

Song No 5

Full chorus number, led by Nurse and Maid Marion, 'Fortuosity' or another

At the end of the song the curtains slowly close

Scene 2

Castle Grounds. An interact scene. May be played in front of tabs or a frontcloth

Sheriff enters one side of the stage. Nickle and Dime enter from the other

Sheriff There you are, you fools. I've been looking for you.
Nickle We've been waiting for ages boss, but they haven't turned up yet.
Sheriff Haven't turned up? What are you talking about? They're in the castle now. They must have walked right past you.
Dime Oh they couldn't have. We're very light sleepers. We'd have woken up.

Nickle gives Dime a kick to shut him up

Sheriff WOKEN UP! You mean you've been asleep! You imbeciles! (*bearing down upon them*) I'm warning you, I can turn very nasty.
Dime (*to audience*) He's started already.

Sheriff Oh yes. I can get very ugly!

Dime (*to audience*) No comment!

Sheriff You're both fired.

Nickle Fired ? You can't fire us - we haven't done anything.

Sheriff That's why I'm firing you!

Nickle We'll talk to our union about this.

Dime Yes, we will. Then they'll come and bash you up.

Sheriff You can't talk to your union.

Nickle Why not?

Sheriff Because they haven't been invented yet, you numbskull!

Dime He's talking to you.

Sheriff You're next to an idiot.

Dime No. He's talking to me.

Sheriff Now listen. I've got an idea. A chance to get your old jobs back. And you won't even have to go into Robin Hood's forest either.

Nickle Right boss, we're listening.

Dime Yes boss, we're all ears.

Nickle You speak for yourself.

Sheriff Be quiet and listen! Now, Nurse Nightingale is going to start a school. So, I want you to disguise yourselves as kids, and go and spy on the Babes.

Nickle What us boss? Go back to school. Oh no, that's kids stuff, that is.

Sheriff Disguise yourselves and go back to school, that's what I said.

Nickle What, and do lessons and things like that?

Dime Here, we won't have to eat school dinners, will we?

Sheriff Never mind about that. I want you to wait for your chance, and, when the opportunity's right (*slit throat action again*) seize it.

Dime (*to Nickle*) What did he say?

Nickle He said when the orange is ripe, squeeze it.

Dime (*puzzled*) Oh.

Sheriff Right. Have you got that?

Dime (*looking round*) No. I haven't got mine boss.

Sheriff Haven't got what?

Dime My orange boss.

Sheriff Orange ? What's he talking about?

Nickle Don't ask me.

Sheriff Streuth! I think I'd better come to this school as well, to keep an eye on you two idiots.

Dime You're not going to disguise yourself as well, are you boss?

Sheriff It looks like I'm going to have to. Come on.

All exit one side, blackout

Scene 3

The Schoolroom. To one side, towards the back of the stage, is a teacher's desk and blackboard. On the blackboard is a face with 'teecher' written under it. Opposite the desk are small, childrens' desks and chairs, or benches. There should be room at the front of the stage for the dancers to perform their dance

On stage is Nurse Nightingale, standing behind her desk

Nurse Enter children.

Chorus of children, with Tom and Mary, enter and stand at front of the stage

Right. Dancing - begin!

Music No 6

A speciality dance number by the junior chorus, dressed as school, or village, children, dancing to a piece of ballet music, or modern pop song. At the end of the number the children sit behind their desks

Nurse Very good children. (*sits down behind her desk*) Now this morning's lesson is all about history. Now, does anyone know what history is?

Chorus 1 puts hand up

Good, someone knows what history is. What is it?
Chorus 1 It's boring miss.

There is a ripple of giggling

Nurse (*standing up*) Be quiet! It's not boring, not the way I do it anyhow. Now, in which battle did Nelson die?
Chorus 2 (*putting hand up*) His last one miss.

Another ripple of giggling

Nurse No! Oh gawd! I need a drink! (*she takes a secret swig at her hip flask*) When I was young I was very good at history.
Chorus 3 But there wasn't much history to learn then, was there?

More giggles, and one or two balls of paper are thrown at her

Nurse I'll start again. Now, where have all the Kings and Queens of England been crowned?

Chorus 4 On their heads miss!

More giggles and thrown paper, as Nickle and Dime enter,, dressed ridiculously as young girls. Dime is pushed on stage, and makes attempts to escape. They stand, feeling stupid, trying to pull their skirts down lower. When the laughter subsides, enter Sheriff, also dressed as a young girl. Nurse comes over to them

Nurse Oh! What's this? More pupils? Well, you're very late. (*looking at the Sheriff*) My! You're a big girl, aren't you? What's your name?

Sheriff (*with a pronounced lisp*) Er, Nellie miss.

Nurse Nellie, eh. You must be Nellie, Nellie with the big fat b....

Sheriff (*forgetting his lisp*) How dare you?

Nurse And how old are you Nellie?

Sheriff (*lisping, holding his skirts and doing a curtsy*) Twelve miss.

Nurse Twelve! You're very big for twelve. You'd better do some skipping.

Sheriff (*in his normal voice*) SKIPPING? What me? (*quickly changing to a lisp*) Er, skipping, what with a rope?

Nurse (*enjoying her joke immensely*) No! Skip breakfast, skip lunch, skip dinner! Ho, ho! Oh, I do tell them! There's life in the old girl yet!

Sheriff (*to audience, doing the fingers across the throat action again*) Not for much longer there won't be.

Nurse You've missed your dancing lesson. You had better do it quickly, now.

Nickle and Dime shake their heads, and make as though to exit. They are stopped by the Sheriff, who is between them and the door

Dime (*in a very squeaky voice*) We can't dance. We're excused dancing (*turning to Nickle*) aren't we Nickle?

Nickle (*also in a squeaky voice*) Yes.

Nurse Nickle?

Nickle Er, I mean, Nicky.

Nurse Have you brought a note to say you are excused dancing, Nicky?

Dime Er, no. We forgot it. But my mum said, didn't she?

Nickle Yes.

Nurse No note? Then you must do your dance.

Dime (*hiding behind Nickle*) No we're shy.

Nurse (*indicating audience*) I bet <u>they</u> want to see you dance, don't you?

Audience (*encouraged by Nurse*) Yes!
Nickle and **Dime** Oh no you don't.
Audience Oh yes we do!
Nickle and **Dime** NO YOU DON'T!
Audience YES WE DO!

This time the Sheriff tries to sneak out. He is stopped by Nickle and Dime

Nickle (*to the Sheriff*) Listen mate, if we've got to dance, so have you.
Sheriff I can't dance. I've got a bad leg. (*he starts to limp in a very exaggerated way, all round the room, groaning as if in agony*)
Nurse Very well then, you can stand on a chair and recite your nine times table.
Sheriff Nine times table? (*to Nickle*) What comes after one nine's nine?
Nickle Search me boss.
Sheriff Streuth, don't you know anything?
Nurse I take it your leg has just made a remarkable recovery?
Sheriff Yes. It's much better, look. (*he gives Nickle a kick*) There you see!
Nurse (*to audience*) Now, let's hear you tell them nice and loud. Do you want to see them dance?
Audience YES !
Sheriff Er! Whose silly idea was this anyway?
Nickle and **Dime** YOURS!

6 maybe me from other script

Music No 7

Nurse sits behind desk, or takes up position to one side of stage. Sheriff, Nickle and Dime, dance a comedy number, 'Three Little Maids from School', from The Mikado. They could also sing the words as they dance. An alternative here would be a dance to a piece of ballet music 'The Sugar Plum Fairy' or another. A routine should be worked out to make this dance as funny as possible. Towards the end of the number, Nickle and Dime stop dancing, unnoticed by the Sheriff, who ends up doing the dance on his own, with Nickle and Dime watching him

At the end of the dance, Sheriff, Nickle and Dime, take up seats at the back. Evicting those already sitting there, who take up seats elsewhere. Sitting immediately in front of the Sheriff are the Babes. The Sheriff takes out a length of rope. and makes as though he is going to strangle Mary

Nurse Nellie! What are you doing with that rope?
Sheriff (*lisping*) Er, I was just going to play conkers miss.

Nurse Put it away! Right then, we will carry on with our history lesson. Now, one of the new girls. When was Shakespeare born?

Nickle and Dime look at each other, hoping for a clue

Dime Er, on his birthday miss?
Nurse Useless!
Dime (*to Nickle*) She's talking to you.

Sheriff takes out dagger, from desk and makes as though about to kill Tom

Nurse What are you doing now Nellie?
Sheriff Er, I'm just going to sharpen my pencil miss.
Nurse Put it away.
Sheriff Cor, she don't let you do nothing, does she?
Nurse Now then, who beat the Philistines?
Nickle We don't know. We don't watch American football.

While this is going on, Sheriff produces an outsize mallet from the desk, and makes as though he is about to hit one of the Babes on the head

Nurse (*seeing the Sheriff about to strike*) WHAT ARE YOU DOING NOW?
Sheriff (*looking guilty*) Er, er, there's a wasp on my desk miss, and I was going to kill it. (*he returns the mallet to the desk*)

At the word 'wasp', the class goes wild and get up, climb on desks etc., and start shouting, 'Help' and 'Where' and 'WASP' etc., Nurse tries to restore order

Nurse Quiet! Sit down and be quiet! (*takes out the hip flask and drinks, and shouts for quiet again, and, getting no response she produces a whistle from her pocket and blows it*) ORDER! ORDER! BACK TO YOUR SEATS!

Order is finally restored

Heavens, it's like the Houses of Parliament in here! Settle down! Now, I've started, so I'll finish, where was I?
Chorus 1 Watching American football!
Nurse Was I? (*going all dreamy*) All those lovely muscly men! (*snapping out of it*) No, I can't have been. Ah yes, history. Now, Nicky, what did Columbus say before he sailed for America?
Dime (*shouting, before Nickle can answer*) ALL ABOARD!

Nurse NO! Oh dear.

Sheriff (*standing up, and using his lisping voice*) Please miss. I know miss.

Nurse (*reassured*) Ah, good. Well done Nellie. And what did Columbus say before he sailed to America?

Sheriff (*doing an Al Jolson imitation, going down on one knee and facing the audience*) Cal-a-fornia, here I come, right back where I started from!

There is uproar again, pupils start to throw paper balls about

Nurse (*blowing whistle and taking out a yellow card which she waves at the Sheriff*) Your last warning! What did Columbus say before he sailed?

Nickle (*standing up, and doing an imitation of the Queen*) He said, 'I name this ship, what's-is-face, and may gawd bless all who sail in her'.

Nurse (*blowing whistle*) That's it! That's it! (*producing red card*) OFF! OFF!

All crowd round Nurse, protesting like angry footballers to a referee, but Nurse insists, pointing at the door. Nickle exits slowly, his head bent down, as Nurse blows whistle pointing at the door. Pupils utter 'Ah' noises as he goes. At the end of this, Sheriff finds mallet and rope, and chases screaming Babes again

Nurse Stop! Stop! What do you think you're doing?

Sheriff (*returning to his desk*) I thought I saw that wasp again, on his head.

Nurse produces a large dunce's hat, and puts it on the Sheriff's head. The pupils laugh and throw paper at him

Nurse Now that's on your head, you numbskull!

Sheriff How dare you! Streuth!

Nurse What?

Sheriff Er, I tell you, it's the truth.

Nurse goes to front of the class. A bell rings. Pupils begin to run off noisily

Nurse Right everyone, It's playtime. Off you go. Not you two (*indicating Sheriff and Dime, who have remained behind*) You'll have to stay in for being naughty gels. (*goes to the door, and calls out*) NICKY !

Nickle (*re-entering the classroom*) Yes, miss.

Nurse Sit down there! And DON'T MOVE!

Nickle sits down. Nurse exits. Sheriff rises and beckons Nickle and Dime to come forward, as curtains close. The rest of the scene is played in front of tabs

Sheriff Come on, let's get out of here, before that old ratbag comes back.

Dime No! We'll get into trouble. She'll give us millions of lines, or make us scrub all the desks, or something.

Sheriff (*to Nickle*) Will you shut him up.

Nickle gives Dime a cuff

Dime Ouch! I'll tell the teacher of you.

Sheriff You fools! You've messed it up again, haven't you?

Dime I say Sheriff, you do look nice! D'you fancy a dance?

Sheriff (*fetching him a blow, so that he ends up on the floor*) Dance, dance? I'll make you dance, if you don't do a bit better than this.

Nickle (*helps Dime up*) Don't blame him. There was no opportunity.

Sheriff You've got to make your own opportunities in life. I didn't get where I am today making excuses. What's happened to our spirit of enterprise, eh?

Nickle (*looking round*) I don't know boss. Where did you leave it last?

Sheriff Double streuth. Perhaps I should send them on a management training course. Look, now you'll have to do the deed tonight.

Nickle Tonight?

Sheriff When everything's quiet, go up to the nursery, and murder them.

Dime Charming!

Nickle Right boss. What about the nurse?

Sheriff That drunken old ratbag. She'll be too sloshed to notice anything.

Dime (*to Nickle*) I read about the evils of drink once.

Nickle Did it cure you?

Dime Oh yes, it cured me alright.

Nickle So you gave up drinking?

Dime No. I gave up reading!

Sheriff Will you shutup? Murder the nurse as well. Then carry them into the forest and bury them.

Dime (*to Nickle*) You can carry her.

Sheriff Make sure you get the job done properly this time, you fools. I must concentrate on the second part of me evil plan. How to get Maid Marion to marry me. Hmm, perhaps I'm using the wrong aftershave?

Nickle Which one is it, Poison?

Sheriff No, Spirit of Cesspool No 5.

Dime What a stinker!

Sheriff Come on - get cracking. There's dirty work to do, up in the nursery.

They all exit. Blackout

Scene 4

Nurse Nightingale's bedroom. To one side is an internal door, leading to Babes'
nursery. Other side a door to the corridor. Centre stage is a bed, with space all
round to move. To one side, near the bed, at the back of the stage, is a screen,
behind which Nurse can 'undress'. Behind the screen is a bundle of clothes,
that will be thrown over the screen by the Nurse

As the curtains open, Nurse is holding a story book and reading to the Babes,
who are in pyjamas, and sitting on the bed. Nurse is wearing a dressing gown
over a full-length nightie, and a night-cap

Nurse   So there was this Little Red Riding Hood, you see, yes, all sweet and
young and innocent, just like me, you see.

Tom   *(yawning)* Haven't you got any Spiderman, or Judge Dredd comics?

Nurse   Spiderman, Judge Fred? Oh no. Nice people don't read those! Anyway I
haven't unpacked mine yet.

Mary   Then can we go to bed now Nurse?

Nurse   Oh, but I haven't finished your nice story yet.

Mary   But you tell us this story every night.

Nurse   It's my favourite. Now, there was a naughty wolf, you see. Big and strong
he was. Oh yes! With a hairy chest, and great big muscles. Isn't it exciting?

Babes settle down to sleep on the nurse's bed, unnoticed by the Nurse

You've never seen such muscles! Then, all of a sudden... *(turns to see Babes*
asleep) All of a sudden they've gone! Well perhaps it's best. If I read any more,
I'll get one of me hot flushes. *(to audience)* Well folks, that's the plot for next
year's panto! So book early, won't you? I wonder if they'll let me be Red Riding
Hood? *(yawns)* What a tiring day! *(settles back and nods off)*

Music No 8

Lights dim for dance from full chorus, or junior chorus. 'Dance of the Toys'.
Chorus dressed as toys and animals etc., Some of the 'toys' may already have
been 'asleep' on stage. Danced to 'March of the Toys' or piece of ballet music, or
modern pop tune. Or, this could be a dance of other pantomime and/or nursery
rhyme characters; Red Riding Hood, the Wolf, Puss in Boots etc.,

At the end of the dance, the lights slowly come up, and, when the applause
has died down, Nurse wakes up abruptly

Nurse Oh dear! I must have dozed off for a moment. Well, what a strange dream! *(gently raises the children from their sleep)*

Babes sleepily get up and go towards their bedroom, guided by Nurse

Nurse *(as they exit)* Say goodnight to the nice people.

Tom and Mary wave to the audience, as they go off. Nurse remains on stage. At the door to the Babes' nursery she calls out

Don't forget to say your prayers now. And sleep tight. *(moves in front of the screen, making as though about to undress)*

*'Stripper' music (**Music No 9**) comes slowly up. Suddenly she remembers that there is an audience there. She puts a protective hand over her bosom*

You must be joking!

'Stripper' music dies. Nurse goes behind the screen, singing `I Feel Pretty' and begins, to throw clothes over the top of the screen, as though she is undressing. The pile mounts, with some curious items; gun and holster, football boots and shirt etc., thrown. Finally the Nurse emerges, dressed exactly as before

There! That's tomorrow's washing sorted! *(pauses as the audience laughs. Looks at them, and at the screen. Realises what they were expecting)* What? You didn't think? Oh no! Not me. Not unless they turn the heating up anyway. *(removes her dressing gown, puts it on the bed, and hops into bed. Shuffles about, then gets out, and kneels beside the bed in prayer)* Oh Lord, I'm so alone and blue. So make the Sheriff love me true. *(makes as though to rise, then adds)* If not, then any man will do. *(gets back into bed)*

The lights slowly dim again. After a short pause, the door to the corridor slowly opens, and Nickle and Dime enter. They talk in loud whispers

Nickle This must be the room. Search round and find the Babes.
Dime It's dark. I can't see a thing. It's like Aladdin's cave.
Nickle Well go and find the little treasures.

Nurse begins to snore

Dime It sounds like the carpenters' shop.

Nickle That'll be the Nurse somewhere, sound asleep.
Nurse (*talking in her sleep*) No, no, Roger Moore, you mustn't!
Dime Ow, er!
Nickle Hasn't got much taste, has she?
Dime Let's go Nick. I don't like the dark.
Nurse No! We hardly know each other!
Dime Oh! Help!
Nickle Come on.

They search round the room and end up bumping, back to back, into each other. Dime yells as they do so

Dime Help!
Nickle Will you be quiet? (*indicating the bed*) Search over there.

They search round the room again. Dime comes to the edge of the bed

Dime (*shouting*) There's something here! (*remembering himself, and whispering*) There's something here.
Nickle (*shouting*) Will you stop shouting? (*whispering*) Will you stop shouting?
Dime You're shouting as well.
Nickle I forgot.
Dime Well I forgot as well.
Nickle You'll get us <u>all</u> murdered, you will. What have you found?
Dime (*feeling around the top of the bed*) I think it's a rhino-rocerus!
Nickle Here, do you know this one? What do they call a short-sighted dinosaur?
Dime Can we go home now?
Nickle No! A 'Do-You-Think-He-Saw-Us'!
Nurse (*turns over, grabs Dime, who is leaning over bed*) Oh alright then Roger, if you insist.
Dime (*struggling to get free*) HELP! Get her off me. I'm suffocating.
Nickle She's only dreaming. Whatever you do, don't wake her up.
Dime What?
Nickle (*shouting*) I said, don't wake her up!
Dime Get her off me!
Nurse (*beginning to stir*) Just one teeny kiss then.
Nickle Now look what you've done.
Nurse (*half awake*) What's that?

Dime struggles free. Nickle and Dime signal to each other to be quiet and wait to see if Nurse goes back to sleep. She seems to settle down again

Nickle Thank goodness for that!

Nurse (*sits upright, wide awake*) OOH - A MAN! TWO MEN! (*gets out of bed*) Thank you Lord! My prayer's answered. Must I choose, or can I have both?

Dime Crikey! Let's get out of here!

Nickle and Dime run round the bed, then round the room, chased by Nurse. Suitable ongoing chase music, crashes etc., here to end of scene

Nurse Come here!

Nickle Where's the door?

Dime Help! MUM!

Nurse (*pausing for breath*) Oh, I wonder which one's Roger Moore?

Nickle and Dime exit on one side of the stage, pursued by the Nurse. They return, run around and across the stage

Dime (*as they cross*) Mercy!

Nurse Come back! Don't be shy. There's only you and me.

Dime If I can find the door, there'll only be you!

Nickle Help! Sheriff, help!

They all exit on the other side. Babes enter from their bedroom, wearing their pyjamas, and rubbing their eyes

Tom Nurse, what's all the noise?

Mary Nurse? Wake up.

They go over to the bed

Tom It's empty. She's not there.

Mary What can have happened to her?

There is the sound of Nickle and Dime shouting off stage

Tom There's someone coming.

Mary Quick let's hide.

They crouch behind bed. Nickle and Dime run on, so scared they seem to be chasing each other. Finally they stop, exhausted, and look at each other

Nickle You're not her.

Dime (*looking down at himself*) No, you're right, I'm not.
Nickle Where is she then?
Dime I don't know.
Nickle Well thank goodness we've lost her.

Enter Sheriff, in nightgown and night cap. He approaches stealthily, looking round, and bumps into Dime

Dime Oh er! She's back! Help!
Nickle (*seeing the Sheriff*) Don't panic, it's only the Sheriff.
Sheriff What do you mean, <u>only</u> the Sheriff? Just watch it!
Nickle Sorry. Sheriff, something nasty's come up.
Sheriff Put some TCP on it then. Have you found them and killed them yet?

Babes look up with fear and surprise on their faces

Nickle Not yet Sheriff. We've had a lot of harassment you see.
Sheriff Don't give me excuses!
Dime We've been chased by the Nurse. She kept shouting for Roger Moore!
Sheriff Roger Moore? Huh. Which one of you is supposed to be Roger Moore?
Dime That's what she kept asking us.
Sheriff Huh. Fancy being afraid of a mere woman.
Dime I'm not afraid. In the army I saved a whole battalion, single handed.
Sheriff How did you do that?
Dime I shot the cook.

Sheriff makes as though he is about to murder Dime. Nurse enters running

Nurse (*stops, puffing and looks round*) I'll head them off at the pass.
Sheriff (*seeing her*) What a sight! Let's get out of here!

Nickle, Dime, and the Sheriff exit

Nurse (*pausing before she chases after them*) Ooh! There's three of them now! (*to the audience*) Isn't it wonderful? I could end up with a whole football team! Wait for me! (*exits same side as Nickle, Dime, and Sheriff*)

The Babes come out from their hiding place

Tom We're in danger Mary.
Mary (*to the audience*) Are we in danger?

Audience Yes.

Mary We'd better do something.

Tom Remember what Marion said. If we were in danger, go to Robin Hood.

Mary (*to the audience*) Can we trust Robin Hood?

Audience Yes.

Mary Are you sure?

Audience YES.

Mary Right. let's go and find him.

Babes exit. Enter Nurse. She stops, puffing and panting

Nurse (*to audience*) Oh my! All this rushing around! I feel just like Anneka Rice! I must rest for a minute. (*sinks back onto the bed*)

Enter the Sheriff, Nickle and Dime. They stop centre stage, puffing

Sheriff I think we've lost her.

Dime Fancy you being scared of a <u>mere</u> woman, Sheriff.

Sheriff Scared? What me? Huh! Nonsense! I always go for a little jog, last thing, before I turn in.

Dime (*disbelieving*) Oh yes.

Sheriff 'Course. It keeps you healthy lad.

Nickle I wonder where she is now?

Dime Miles away, I hope.

Nickle (*indicating the audience*) Perhaps they know. Shall we ask them?

Nurse sits up on the bed

Sheriff Go on then, ask them. About time they did something useful.

Nickle Which way did she go?

Audience She's behind you!

Sheriff No, no. Don't mess about. Which way did the old ratbag go?

Audience She's behind you.

Nickle No, she can't be. You're just trying to make us look round.

Sheriff Next time I see her, I'll show her who's boss. Come on, where is she?

Audience She's behind you.

Nurse gets up and creeps up on them. Dime looks round and sees her

Dime Oh, er! (*tugs at Nickle's sleeve, and points to behind him*) Nick, Nick!

Nickle (*to Dime*) Now <u>you're</u> trying to scare me as well, aren't you?

Dime No, look!

They finally look round, see the Nurse, and run off stage again, shouting help etc., Nurse, gleefully, chases after them. Enter Maid Marion, on the corridor side, wearing a dressing gown

Maid Marion I heard a commotion. I thought I had better check that the Babes are alright. *(exits to the nursery, and quickly returns)* They've gone! Where can they be? *(goes to the Nurse's bed)* Nurse has gone too! I'm sure something dreadful has happened. *(to audience)* Has something dreadful happened?

Audience Yes.

Maid Marion Oh dear. I knew it. Is it something to do with the Sheriff?

Audience Yes.

Maid Marion He - he hasn't - hurt them, has he?

Audience No.

Maid Marion Well thank goodness for that anyway. Where are they then?

Audience Run away. Gone to find Robin. Run to the forest. etc.,

Maid Marion Gone to the forest?

Audience Yes.

Maid Marion Gone to the forest, on their own. I must hurry and find them. *(makes to exit)*

Nurse *(running on)* Where are they?

Maid Marion Nurse! There you are. Where have you been?

Nurse *(collecting herself)* What? Oh, it's you Maid Marion. I wasn't expecting to find you here. *(looks around the stage for the men)* Which way did they go?

Maid Marion They've run off to the forest.

Nurse Run off to the forest! I'm not chasing them all over there!

Maid Marion The Babes have run off to get away from the Sheriff.

Nurse What? Oh, I see. And the Sheriff's run off to get away from me!

Maid Marion What?

Nurse I said, 'A dreadful thing to live to see'.

Maid Marion What have you been doing?

Nurse What? Oh, it was those men, you see.

Maid Marion Have they been chasing you as well?

Nurse Oh no, I've been chas... chas... Er, well, yes of course, that's it. Those dreadful men, Parsley and Thyme...

Maid Marion Nickle and Dime.

Nurse That's what I said dear, Reason and Rhyme. Yes. They've been chasing me all over. Oh a terrible time I've had. You wouldn't believe. *(to audience)* Haven't I been chased all over by those dreadful men?

Audience NO!

Nurse You be quiet, you lot. It's past your bed-times anyway.

Maid Marion We must do something.

Nurse Yes. Send them all home.

Maid Marion NO! About the Babes I mean.

Nurse Oh, the Babes, yes. (*produces handkerchief, and going into an exaggerated show of concern*) Oh me poor Babes! (*walking round the stage*) Me little darlings! Where are you I'll kill the Sheriff with my bare hands, if anything's happened to them. Oh, so innocent, not knowing the wicked ways of the world...

Maid Marion Yes, they were.

Nurse Not them - ME! I should have known! 'Beware the Sheriff' - don't you see. The Fairy Queen <u>was</u> trying to warn me! I knew it was a message. 'Go and hide in the dustbin,' she said. 'And don't look at the Sheriff's hideous behind.'

Maid Marion (*confused*) What?

Nurse Oh yes, I knew. I'm very psycho-sematic, you know.

Maid Marion I always told them to find Robin Hood, if they were in danger. I hope that's where they've gone.

Nurse Let's look for them in the forest then.

Both exit. Enter Nickle and Dime, followed by the Sheriff, who is hitting them

Sheriff You useless fools! You've let them get away again! Can't you do anything right? Frightened by a feeble old woman. You should be ashamed of yourselves. Go and find them. And don't come back this time without them. (*exits*)

Nickle What a life! We were better off when we were being chased by nurse. (*thinks for a moment, then shakes his head*) No we weren't. Come on.

Dime So it's back to the forest then.

Nickle Yes. I'm afraid so.

Dime Good I'm glad you're afraid as well. I know a song about Robin Hood. Can we sing it? I need a song to cheer me up.

Nickle Good idea. Let's get these people down here to sing it as well.

Song No 10

Community song. The words may be provided on a board

> Robin Hood, Robin Hood,
> Riding through the glen.
> Robin Hood, Robin Hood,
> With his band of men.
> Feared by the bad, loved by the good.
> Robin Hood, Robin Hood, Robin Hood.

At the end of the first attempt, the Sheriff enters

Sheriff What's going on here?
Nickle We were getting these people to sing about Robin Hood.
Sheriff He's that soppy outlaw! I know a better song about him.

The alternative version is brought on.

> Robin Hood, Robin Hood,
> Spies the Weetabix.
> Robin Hood, Robin Hood,
> Now he's in a fix.
> Should he return, back to Sherwood?
> 'Course he should, 'course he should, 'course he should!

At the end of the song, all exit. Curtain

Interval

ACT 2

Scene 1

A Clearing in Sherwood Forest. There should, if possible, be a mound towards the back of the stage, where the Babes can fall asleep. Also, there should be somewhere, a tree or space by the wings, for Nickle, Dime, and the Sheriff to hide. It is an hour or so since the Babes ran away, and late evening, so the level of lighting should indicate this

Enter the Babes, Tom entering first

Tom Come on Mary.
Mary Oh Tom, can't we stop now? I'm so tired.
Tom Just a little further.

They exit across the stage. After a brief pause they enter again

Mary (*looking round*) I think we've been past this bit. (*sitting down on the mound*) We're going round in circles. I can't go any further.
Tom Alright. We'll rest here for a while. (*sits on the mound as well*) Then we must move on, and try to find Robin Hood. (*heroically*) You go to sleep, I'll stay awake and keep guard.

Mary lies down and falls asleep. A moment later Tom lies back and falls asleep as well. To a tinkling of bells, enter the Fairy Queen and Firefly. Firefly encourages the audience to shout, as usual

Audience Oh come on Fairy Queen, get cracking!
Sunny Spells Fear not, brave Babes, enjoy your hour of slumber.
My forest troupe will dance a magical, sweet number.
To ward away the evil, and the bad,
And cheer your sleep with dreams that make you glad.
We will watch o'er you, guard you through the night.
Our power for good upholds the cause of right.

The Fairy Queen waves her wand, and the dancers enter

Music No 11

*Traditional dance of the forest creatures; animals, fairies, forest goblins etc.,
This dance may be performed under a fluorescent UV lamp, which is most
effective if a quantity of white is to be worn by the dancers. To a suitable piece
of ballet music, or whatever, the creatures appear carrying leaves, and dance
around, and in front of, the sleeping Babes. They place leaves over the Babes
as they dance. Fairy Queen, and Firefly, may be included in the dance. Or they
may stand at the side of the stage, and overlook the proceedings*

*At the end of the dance, Sunny Spells and Firefly come to the centre of the
stage. The dancers group around them, listening, agreeing, and laughing.*

Firefly (*to audience*) She's back to her normal self again, thank goodness! (*to
Fairy Queen*) You see how good you can be when you are really trying..

Sunny Spells I can't stand by and watch this. We must do something to protect
these poor little waifs. (*carried away, walking up and down*) Left out in the
dreadful forest all night! That awful Sheriff, I'll throttle him when I find him...

Firefly Yes, alright Fairy Queen, don't get carried away. (*to audience*) Perhaps I
spoke too soon! (*to the Fairy Queen*) Fairy Queens don't throttle people, it's
not their way. They just sort of stand all dignified, like this see, and wave their
wands, (*she goes through the actions as though she is auditioning for the part
of Fairy Queen*) and something wonderful happens. Didn't you see Pinocchio?

Sunny Spells Pinocchio! Huh! You call her a fairy queen! I seem to remember
that Pinocchio was 'wonderfully' turned into a donkey, with a huge wooden
nose, and ended up inside a whale! Some Fairy Queen! They threw her out of
the union you know. Oh, yes. It caused quite a stir at the time. She never
worked for Disney again, after that. Well, it gives the NAF's a very bad name.

Firefly NAF's?

Sunny Spells National Association of Fairies. We senior Fairy Queen's have our
standards to keep up you know.

Firefly Yes, yes! Don't get carried away again.

Sunny Spells Don't get carried away? (*Scots accent*) Those poor wee, wee bairns,
left oot here to freeze, and aw you can think aboot is Pinocchio.

Firefly She does accents too! Look, we'll settle for you just being a normal Fairy
Queen.

Sunny Spells Hmm, something's certainly got to be done about that dreadful
Sheriff. I hope I don't have to use one of my Number One Spells, from my Big
Bumper Book of Spells.

All on stage gasp at the thought of this

Firefly The Big Bumper Book?

Sunny Spells Yes, well, we shall see. Come on, let's go and do some planning.

Firefly Right.

Chorus nod agreement as they exit to a tinkling of bells. Firefly and Sunny Spells exit. As Sunny Spells goes, she pauses, with a devilish glint

Sunny Spells Oh yes. We'll put that nasty Sheriff in a fix.
                          But now it's time to have our cup of Horlicks! *(exits)*

Firefly *(to audience)* Sorry about that. I wish I'd auditioned for the part myself now! If Andrew Lloyd Webber is watching we'll never get to Broadway! *(exits)*

Lights slowly come up. It is morning. Sound effects of bird-song can indicate this. The Babes wake up yawning, Tom first

Tom Mary, it's morning. We'd better be going.

Mary Yes Tom. *(sitting up)* Did you stay awake and keep watch then?

Tom Er, yes, of course!

Mary I had such a strange dream! The forest was full of fairies and animals, all taking care of us. They covered us with leaves. *(she notices the leaves over her)* Oh! How strange?

Tom Never mind that now. Let's go.

Both get up and exit. Desmond enters from the other side and watches them go. A brief pause, and then Maid Marion and Robin Hood enter behind Desmond

Robin Hood The Babes ran away from the castle you say?

Maid Marion The Sheriff was after them. They must have come into the forest.

Robin Hood Well, don't worry. With the help of my Merry Men we'll soon find them. My men and I know every inch of this forest. *(seeing Desmond)* And here's Desmond, he can help us look for the Babes as well.

Maid Marion Will you help us to look for the Babes?

Desmond nods affirmatively

Good. Which way shall we look first?

Desmond points in the direction that the Babes went

Robin Hood Right. We'll look over there first.

Robin and Marion exit in the direction indicated. Enter Nurse, exhausted and puffing. Desmond looks at her with some curiosity

Nurse Oh dear! They're going too fast for me. I can't keep up with them. (*to audience*) Which way did they go?

The audience will indicate the direction that Robin and Marion have gone

Over there? Right. Oh, a horse! Perhaps he'll give me a lift. Shall I ask him?
Audience Yes.
Nurse Right. I will. (*to Desmond*) Here horsey, nice horsey. Will you give me a ride over there?

Desmond backs away and shakes his head

Oh, go on. I'm ever so tiny and light really.

Desmond shakes his head again

I think he means yes. Come on now. Steady etc.,

Nurse proceeds to move round Desmond, appealing to him, and looking for an opportunity to climb onto Desmond's back. She makes some attempts to climb on, but meets with strong resistance. Finally she is thrown to the floor with her legs in the air, to screams of 'Oh' and 'help' etc., Desmond runs off the stage

(*picking herself up*) I'll say a rude word to him, next time I see him. Yes. Venison! That's what I'll say. Now I'll have to walk. Oh dear, I hope we find those poor Babes soon. (*exits in the same direction as Robin and Marion*)

Enter the Merry Men

Friar Tuck Have any of you seen Robin Hood this morning?

The Merry Men shake their heads, and look at each other

Little John He just had three shredded wheats, as usual, and went off early.
Much Ow, ah!
Will I expect his girlfriend's come round.
Much Come round? Why, was she unconscious?
Will Much - a word in your ear (*puts mouth to Much's ear*) BOO!

Much (*as he jumps*) OIY!

Will I could see daylight right through there!

Little John (*to Friar Tuck, pointing at Much*) His lift doesn't go to the top floor.

Much Why are you lot always picking on me?

Will Because you cook breakfast in your pyjamas.

Much Ow, ah. What's wrong with that?

Will You should use the frying-pan, like everyone else.

All laugh at this

Tom Farrier The lady from the farm brought round a chicken to cook, yesterday.

They all look at each other and groan

Will (*to Friar Tuck*) Another one of his jokes coming up.

Tom Farrier So I said to her, we don't want this, it's frozen. So she said...

Everyone on stage, except Tom Farrier, finishes the last line

Will, Friar Tuck etc So would you be with no feathers on.

Tom Farrier Oh! Have you heard it?

Will Only a hundred times.

General laughs

Friar Tuck It's so quiet and peaceful here. No panic or stress. Just relaxing,

Little John And fishing,

Friar Tuck And eating...

Little John (*tapping Friar Tuck's large stomach*) Trust you to think of food.

Friar Tuck Then more relaxing...

Will And more eating, and more fishing...

Song No 12

Merry Men sing. 'Busy Doing Nothing' or 'Gone Fishing' or 'I Love those Lazy, Hazy Days of Summer' or another. Village and forest folk could come on, to make this a full chorus number

At the end of the song

Little John Ah yes! It's always so peaceful in the forest.

Will Scarlet No panic.
Friar Tuck No hurry.
Much Ow, ah. No worry, nor nothing.
Little John Just the gentle warbling of the birds. Listen, can you hear?

All listen. Off stage Robin is heard to call 'Hurry, hurry. Hurry, hurry'

Friar Tuck Eh, what kind of bird is that?
Much That be the 'hurry, hurry' bird. Very rare in these parts.

Enter Robin and Marion

Robin Hood (*excited*) Ah there you are. We've been looking all over for you. We've got urgent work to do.
Maid Marion Yes, quick. We've got to save the Babes, hurry.

Enter Nurse, running

Nurse Haven't you found the Babes yet? What are you all standing around doing nothing for?
Will (*steps forward*) So, who mentioned peace and quiet, and ruined everything?
Little John and **Friar Tuck** (*together, pointing to Much*) It was him.
Robin Hood Now listen Men. This is serious. The Babes have run away from the castle, because they are in danger from the Sheriff. We must find them, and protect them.
Merry Men (*serious now*) Right Robin. Yes Robin. What shall we do? etc.,
Little John What do you want us to do Robin?
Robin Hood Little John, You take some men and search the north side, the rest come with me to the south. We <u>must</u> find them before the Sheriff's men..
Little John Right.
Much Ow, ah.

Robin Hood, Maid Marion and Friar Tuck exit on one side. Little John, Will Scarlet exit on the other. Leaving Much the Miller and Nurse on stage.

Nurse (*to audience*) All those lovely men! Which one shall I choose?
Much (*sidling up to her*) Ow, ah. Hello darlin. How's about you and me having a little get together then, eh?
Nurse (*to audience*) Well, I'm not choosing this one, that's for sure. Phew! If this was Aladdin, he'd be High Pong. (*to Much*) How dare you! I'll 'ave you know you are in the presence of a 'ighly respectable woman.

Much   (*looking round*) Ow, ah. Respectable woman. Where?

Nurse   (*outraged*) OH! (*hitting him*) I am - you fool!

Much   Ow, ah. That's a funny name, 'You fool'.

Nurse   What?

Much   You said, 'I am 'you fool', and I said...

Nurse   Oh don't bother to explain it, we'll be here all night. They call you Jack Russell, I suppose - cos you're barking?

Much   What? No, I'm Much.

Nurse   Much? How much?

Much   Much the Miller. But they call me Not Much, for some reason.

Nurse   I can't think why.

Much   I've got me own mill. You know that song, 'There's an old mill by the stream'. It's written about my mill you see. Not a lot of people know that.

Nurse   How excruciatingly, painfully interesting. (*looking at his neck*) Anyway, what's that growth on your neck?

Much   Oh that. That's me head.

Nurse   You should see a doctor about it. Get it amputated.

Much   No. Doctors are no good. I went to a doctor once.

Nurse   To have the smell surgically removed?

Much   What? No. I said to him, 'Doctor. I keep thinking I'm an apple pie'.

Nurse   What happened?

Much   He poured custard all over me, and bit me arm!

Nurse   How revolting! Was he poisoned?

Much   Ow, ah. Then I had to tell him about me memory, you see.

Nurse   You told him you could remember being a human being once?

Much   What? No, not that far back, no. I told him, 'Doctor, doctor, I keep losing me memory.' So he said, 'How long's this been going on?' So I said, 'How long's what been going on?' and he told me to hop it. Didn't give me no anti-bionic tablets for it, nor nothing.

Nurse   (*yawns*) Riveting stuff.

Much   So he asked me how old I was. I told him I couldn't remember that neither. But, I said, if I'd known how long I was going to live, I'd have looked after meself a bit better. So he said, I had a case of amnesia. 'I have not,' I said, 'I don't drink it. I only drink cider'. Let's you and me sing a song.

Nurse   Ow, ah. Ow, ah!

Song No 13

Comedy song and dance, 'How you Gonna Keep 'em Down on the Farm' or 'Old MacDonald had a Farm' or 'Tit Willow' or another

If the former is chosen, the following words are suggested

> How you gonna keep me/him down on the farm,
> Now that I've/he's seen Nursey?
> How you gonna keep me/him turning mill-stones,
> After she's gone, after she's gone? I ask ya.
> How you gonna keep me/him on my/his own?
> That's the mystery.
> The turning arms of windmills, they may have their charms.
> But I'd/he'd prefer the charms of dear old Nursey's arms.
> So, how you gonna keep me/him down on the farm,
> Now that I've/he's seen Nursey?
>
> How you gonna keep me/him in the countryside,
> Now that I've/he's seen Nursey?
> How you gonna keep me/him with ducks and chickens,
> If she's not there, if she's not there? I ask ya.
> How you gonna keep me/him on my/his own?
> I'd/he'd be a misery.
> The country birds make music, but to no avail.
> Cos it isn't like the singing of this Nightingale.
> So, how you gonna keep me/him down on the farm,
> Now that I've/he's seen Nursey?

At the end of the song, Will Scarlet returns

Will *(to Much)* Come on you. There's work to do. *(drags Much off the stage)*

Nurse Well! Thank goodness that's over. Tune in again next week for another exciting episode of 'Emmerdale Farm'.

Nurse exits in the direction of Robin and Marion. Enter Sheriff, Nickle and Dime

Dime It's like looking for a needle in a haystack, boss.

Nickle Yea, two needles in a haystack.

Sheriff You useless pair. You couldn't find a haystack in a matchbox. If we don't find them, and do the bizz, *(finger across throat again)* you can forget that trip to EuroDisney I promised you.

Dime Ow boss!

Sheriff Shh. I hear someone coming. Hide quickly.

They scramble to hide behind the tree, or in the wings, getting in each other's way etc., when they are settled, enter the Babes from the opposite side

Mary We've walked for miles and we haven't seen anybody.
Tom Well at least we haven't seen the Sheriff or his men.

Dime wanders out from the tree, and is pulled back to cover by Nickle

Sheriff The fool! I'll kill him!
Mary Listen. Did you hear something?
Tom No.
Mary I'm scared. (*to audience*) You will tell us if you see the Sheriff, won't you?
Audience He's behind you etc.,
Mary What?

They look round, but see nothing

Tom There's no-one there. It's just the shadows of the trees.
Mary (*to audience*) Did you really see him?

Sheriff appears and seems ready to pounce. Then hides again

Audience He's behind you!

Babes look round, but see nothing. This can continue as long as desired. Then, finally the Sheriff, Nickle and Dime pounce

Sheriff Grab them men!

Nickle and Dime hold Babes secure, after struggle and shouting from Babes

Good, you're in me power. Don't kill 'em yet. I've thought of a plan to get Maid Marion to marry me. I'll tell her I won't kill them, if she'll agree to marry me.
Nickle Good. That's very generous of you boss.
Sheriff Then I'll kill them anyway, after the wedding.
Nickle I take back what I said!
Dime Oh, but that's telling lies, that is!
Sheriff Lies? What you talking about? That's strategy! You'll never make a politician, you won't. (*to audience*) Don't you think I'm great?
Audience No!
Sheriff I wonder if there's an opening for me in the cabinet?

Dime Dunno. But there's a big rat-hole behind the toilet.

Sheriff With brains like mine, I should be Prime Minister!

Nickle There's a joke in there somewhere as well!

Sheriff Oh yes I should!

Audience Oh no you shouldn't.

Sheriff Yes I should!

Audience No you shouldn't!

Sheriff Take them away and stick 'em in the dungeon.

Dime (*looking, and pointing at the audience*) What, all of them?

Sheriff Not them! These two!

Nickle Right boss.

Nickle and Dime take the Babes off as they struggle

Sheriff Now, I wonder where that useless Robin Hood is. I can't wait to tell him the good news. Cheer him up a bit. Ha, ha! I'll see if he's hiding in his den. (*to audience*) I've won, so you might as well all go home. Yes I have.

Audience No you haven't.

Sheriff Don't start that again. (*exits*)

Enter Robin and Marion and Merry Men who move forward as the curtains slowly close, or a frontcloth showing another part of the forest is flown

Little John It's hopeless Robin, we've searched everywhere.

Robin Hood We'll go back to the camp, to see if there's any news. You lot continue searching. Come on Marion, don't give up yet.

Exit Robin Hood and Maid Marion

Friar Tuck We can't search any more, we're exhausted.

Little John Right. Let's be methodical about this.

Will Scarlet Metho-logical. That's a good word. I wish I was educated.

Much Ow, ah.

Little John I mean, where have we looked so far. Then we will know where we still have to look. Now, where have you looked Will?

Will Scarlet I searched the village - not a sausage.

Friar Tuck Down in the cutting - there was nuttin'.

Tom Farrier Over the hill - it was all very still.

Friar Tuck Down in the meadow - not even a shadow.

Will Scarlet I went to the farm - and raised the alarm.

Much I went to the dell - they told me to go to - look somewhere else.

Little John Right. So where does that leave us?

Tom Farrier Standing here.

Friar Tuck We could look in the pub.

Little John No. They won't be there.

Friar Tuck No. But we could have a beer, couldn't we?

Little John You and your stomach!

Will Perhaps the Sheriff's already got them, and killed them.

Little John (*shocked*) Don't say that, it's bad luck.

Will You don't believe all that superstitious stuff do you?

Tom Farrier I do.

Little John Really?

Tom Farrier I knew a bloke walked under a ladder once.

Will signals for them all to finish the last line of the joke again

Will (*innocently*) Really. What happened?

Tom Farrier Well...

Will, Little John etc Forty three years later, all his teeth fell out.

Tom Farrier Oh! Have you heard it?

Will That joke's so old, it's moved to Eastbourne.

Little John So has that one too. Now we must get organised. We'll never find these Babes if we don't.

Will Yes, alright Field Marshall.

Little John Now my plan is this.

They gather round expecting some clever plan

Er, we'll just have to look everywhere again.

General shock at this. Cries of 'What' and 'You're joking' etc

Friar Tuck We need a rest.

Will Some peace and quiet.

Friar Tuck And some food.

Tom Farrier A nice laze in the sun.

Song No 14

Chorus number from the Merry Men. This may be a short reprise of 'I Love Those Lazy, Hazy Days of Summer' (Song No 12) Or a new song

At the end of the song they all exit, blackout

Scene 2

Robin Hood's Forest Camp. An untidy collection of equipment, junk, cooking utensils, weaponry etc., is littered round the stage. There is a notice on a tree

Sheriff *(entering)* So this is it. The famous Robin Hood's camp. I wonder what Community Charge he pays for this? Nobody around eh? Let's see what valuables he's got lying around. *(seeing notice)* What's this? 'This is a Neighbourhood Watch Area - so don't try and nick nothing.' Huh, nothing worth nicking anyway. What a stupid idea, rob the rich, feed the poor. He'll never make a Chancellor of the Exchequer.

Enter Robin Hood, Maid Marion and the Merry Men

Robin Hood There he is men! The wicked Sheriff. Seize him.
Little John Right Robin.

The Merry Men surround the Sheriff, some holding him secure

Sheriff Take your hands off me. I'm the Sheriff, you fools!
Robin Hood Not for long. You're very foolish, coming to my camp, alone.
Tom Farrier Full of bravery or...
Merry Men Carling Black Label.
Sheriff Yes, well, heroes run in my family - fast! Ha, ha!
Robin Hood Thank goodness the Babes managed to escape from you.
Sheriff Ah, but they didn't!
Robin Hood What?

There is general shock and concern at this

Sheriff You heard, cloth-ears. Even as we speak they are playing 'Dragons and Dungeons' in their very own dungeon. Ha! Release me, or you'll be sorry.
Robin Hood Release him.

Those holding the Sheriff let him go

Sheriff *(brushes himself down)* That's better. Now. The Babes are held by my men. Unless Maid Marion agrees to marry me, you will never see them again! Ha! *(to audience)* Not a bad panto. Could have written it myself! Yes I could!

Audience No you couldn't.

Sheriff Ha! It's time the baddies won for a change! Yes I will.

Audience No you won't.

Sheriff Yes I will.

Audience No you won't.

Sheriff Just watch me. *(looks at Marion and Robin, who are very sad as Robin tries to comfort Marion)* Look at them. Look like they've won a free holiday to Outer Mongolia! Ha! Charles Bronson's *(or current TV baddie)* got nothing on me. *(struts round like a gun-slinger)* I'll give you 'til sundown to make up your mind. Oh I can be cruel. They don't call me the Robert Maxwell of Nottingham for nothing. See you all at the wedding folks. Bring plenty of expensive presents. *(to audience)* Told you I'd won. You wouldn't listen. *(exits, laughing)*

Maid Marion Well Robin. I have no choice. You know what I must say?

Robin Hood Yes Marion. We can't let anything bad happen to the Babes.

Maid Marion I'm sorry Robin.

Robin Hood Cheer up. At least you'll be able to keep an eye on the Babes.

Song No 15

This may be a down-tempo reprise of the love duet Song No 2. Or it can be another sad love song, 'This Nearly was Mine' or 'Somewhere' or another. The Merry Men may remain and form a chorus around Marion and Robin, or they may exit, leaving Maid Marion and Robin Hood alone, when the Sheriff exits

At the end of the song

Maid Marion Goodbye Robin.

Robin Hood Goodbye Marion.

Marion exits on the same side as the Sheriff. Robin is left alone on stage. He shuffles about, then, to a tinkling of bells, enter Sunny Spells and Firefly, unseen by Robin Hood. Firefly urges the audience to shout

Audience Come on Fairy Queen, get cracking!

Sunny Spells 'Tis Robin Hood, our hero, looking sad.
What can have happened that could be so bad?

Firefly Let's make ourselves visible to him and find out.

Sunny Spells On very rare occasions, you are right,
We can appear to mortals in a plight.
But it's a special privilege, you see,
And something to be used most sparingly.

Firefly Come on Fairy Queen. This looks urgent. (*to audience*) Is it urgent?
Audience Yes!
Sunny Spells Oh very well, we'll break the rules this time.
And no doubt hear of the Sheriff's latest crime.
(*waving wand*)
Robin! Attend! And tell us what's amiss.
What evil deed can make you look like this?
Robin Hood (*now looking round and seeing the Fairy Queen*) What? Who's
that? I thought I was alone.
Firefly What is it Robin? We're here to help you. This is your Fairy Queen.
Robin Hood Fairy Queen? Really!
Firefly (*to Fairy Queen*) Isn't he nice? He looks so sad and vulnerable! I see
what you mean now, about being good all the time having its drawbacks. (*she
goes over to Robin Hood and smiles sweetly at him*)
Sunny Spells Firefly! Come back here and behave yourself! Well! You've grown
up quickly, I must say! (*wryly*) You'll never get to be a Fairy Queen that way!
Firefly (*returning shame-faced to the Fairy Queen*) Sorry Fairy Queen.
Sunny Spells Now Robin, you must speak to us. What is it?
Robin Hood The Sheriff has taken the Babes captive. He's forcing Marion to
marry him, or he'll do something terrible to them.
Firefly WHAT!
Sunny Spells I don't believe it! I don't know what the world's coming to. Thank
goodness I didn't retire and take up gardening. The petunias will have to wait.
Well, there's nothing for it but a Number One Spell from the Bumper Book. let
me see. (*very serious now, as a spell is prepared, with waving of wand, to
suitable sound and lighting effects*)
Sheriff Stoneyheart of Nottingham, beware!
For now I must a punishment prepare.
Something that suits your wretched infamy.
Behave like a beast - then a beast you now shall be!
(*the spell is suitably rounded off with a flash*)
Firefly (*excited and bewildered*) Good gracious! (*looking round*) What has
happened? What have you done?
Sunny Spells (*to Robin*) You have a deer, I believe. Desmond by name. He was
illtreated by the Sheriff. Is this not so?
Robin Hood Yes Fairy Queen, you're right.
Sunny Spells Of course I am. Well! I have just arranged for the Sheriff and
Desmond to change places for a while.
Firefly WHAT!
Sunny Spells Let the Sheriff find out what it is like to be a real beast.

Robin Hood I say! You mean that the Sheriff has changed into Desmond, and Desmond has changed into the Sheriff?

Sunny Spells Yes. Just one more chapter in the endless fight against crime.

Robin Hood I'd really like to see that. (*to audience*) Would you like to see that?

Audience Yes.

Sunny Spells Very well. And so you shall. (*calls to off-stage*) Sheriff, come here.

Sheriff (*off*) No!

Sunny Spells (*more sternly*) Sheriff, come here!

Sheriff (*off*) No! I won't.

Sunny Spells Now you don't want anything worse to happen, do you?

The deer enters slowly. The Sheriff can have taken up a place as the front-half of the deer, during his absence from stage. Or he can call his lines from the wings, as the deer reacts on stage. Those on stage laugh as he shuffles on

Sheriff (*to the audience*) It's rude to laugh at people's afflictions. (*to Sunny Spells*) Let me out of here! You can't do this to the Sheriff!

Sunny Spells Oh yes I can.

Sheriff Oh no you can't.

Sunny Spells (*encouraging the audience to join in*) Oh yes I can - and have.

Firefly Is that you Sheriff? It's not a fancy dress party, you know.

Sheriff This is very embarrassing. (*to Fairy Queen*) Here, you're not Jeremy Beadle in disguise, are you?

Sunny Spells NO!

Firefly Sheriff! You don't look very well today - MY DEER!

Sheriff (*he thrashes about as though attempting to get out of his skin*) Streuth and double streuth! What sort of a trick do you call this? Let me out at once!

Sunny Spells You wanted to behave like a beast, well, now you can. In fact Desmond is much better behaved than you. He will make a very good Sheriff.

Firefly Yes. I agree.

Sheriff Who asked you! Will you let me out of here?

Sunny Spells (*to audience*) Shout 'Yes' if you want Desmond to stay the Sheriff.

Audience YES!

Sunny Spells There. You see.

Sheriff Be quiet you horrible lot.

Robin Hood Well! That's not very nice! Desmond wouldn't behave like that.

Sheriff (*changing tack*) Come on Fairy Queen. You've had your little joke.

Sunny Spells You don't want to be Desmond any more?

Sheriff No. Change me back - please!

Sunny Spells Well, I don't know. (*turning to Firefly*) What do you think?

Firefly (*shaking her head*) I don't know. Robin?

Robin Hood Hmm. It'll take some thinking about.

Sheriff (*losing temper*) WILL YOU STOP MESSING ABOUT! (*remembers himself*) I mean, I won't be bad any more. Honest. Cross me heart and hope to die.

Sunny Spells Really? Is that a promise?

Sheriff Yes, I promise.

Sunny Spells (*to audience*) Can we trust him, do you think?

Audience No!

Sheriff Don't ask them!

Sunny Spells Perhaps you have learnt your lesson. Go back to the castle now. As soon as the Babes are released, you will become your normal self again.

Sheriff (*making to exit*) Alright.

Sunny Spells (*stopping him*) Just a moment. I haven't finished.

Sheriff Yes, what is it you silly old... Er, I mean, was there something else Fairy Queen?

Sunny Spells You must agree to the marriage of Maid Marion to Robin Hood.

Sheriff Oh no, not that, please, must I?

Sunny Spells (*to audience*) Yes?

Audience YES!

Sheriff Streuth! Alright then. (*makes to exit again*)

Sunny Spells AND!

Sheriff (*stopping*) What else?

Sunny Spells You must hand over everything to the Babes. The castle and all your titles and possessions.

Sheriff What! You must be joking!

Sunny Spells (*making preparations with the wand*) Another spell, I think. Perhaps he'd like to be a snail for a while?

Sheriff No! Streuth! Alright. (*making to go again*)

Sunny Spells ONE LAST LITTLE THING.

Sheriff I don't believe it. What else can there be?

Sunny Spells As you were so keen to marry, you must find someone to marry you - before midnight - or go back to what you are. That should keep you busy.

Sheriff Before midnight? I'm not Cinderella you know! Who'll want to marry me, when I'm poor? Even I wouldn't want to marry me!

Firefly A stroke of genius, Fairy Queen! You <u>really</u> got cracking!

Sunny Spells Off you go now.

Sheriff I don't suppose one of you two ladies would care to, I mean, to get married, perhaps? Make an honest man of me, eh?

Sunny Spells Huh! Now <u>you</u> must be joking! Off now.

Sheriff (*makes to go, but suspects there is something else*) You sure there's nothing else?

Sunny Spells No. Off you go, before I change my mind.

Sheriff/Desmond hurries off. The Merry Men come back on

Little John What's happening Robin?
Will Why is Desmond behaving so strangely?
Robin Hood Well, he's not himself, at the moment.
Much Ow, ah. Ow, ah.
Tom Farrier Reminds me of a joke...
Friar Tuck Not now Tom.

More villagers come on, asking questions, if Song No 16 is a big chorus number

Robin Hood Poor Sheriff! I feel almost sorry for him. Thank you Fairy Queen
for all your kindness. I feel like singing a song.
Sunny Spells We thought you would.

Song No 16

*Full chorus number, led by Robin Hood, 'If I were a Bell, I'd be Ringing' or 'On
a Wonderful Day Like Today' or another. Fairy Queen and Firefly can take up
places on either side of the stage and observe, or simply stand on either side of
Robin, and join in the singing*

At the end of the song

Robin Hood Now please excuse me. I must go to the castle to find Marion.
Sunny Spells Goodbye Robin, and good luck.

Robin and chorus exit, as all wave him goodbye and good luck etc

Not bad for a day's work!
Firefly (*as she exits*) Didn't she do well?

Sunny Spells and Firefly exit, to tinkling of bells. Blackout and Curtain

Scene 3

*A Castle Dungeon. This can be performed in front of tabs, in a spotlight, with
dim general lighting, or using a frontcloth. On stage when the curtains open
are the Babes and Maid Marion, huddled together in a corner, sitting on stools,
or on the floor. If in front of tabs, they walk on*

Maid Marion Now you mustn't worry. Everything's going to be alright. We'll be out of this terrible dungeon soon. If I agree to marry the Sheriff, then I can stay here and look after you.

Mary But you mustn't marry the Sheriff just for our sake. He's horrible!

Tom We were right not to like him, when we arrived.

Enter Nickle, carrying a piece of paper, and Dime

Nickle There's something funny happening to the Sheriff.

Dime He's making very strange noises, and he keeps asking for hay to eat.

Nickle And galloping around the hall.

Maid Marion Heavens! Perhaps all that badness has turned to madness.

Nickle (*shows paper to Marion*) He's written a note.

Dime He didn't half have trouble holding the pen though.

Nickle It says the Babes are to be released immediately.

Dime He says he wants be a deer again. Whatever that means.

Maid Marion He never was a dear.

Nickle You're not really going to marry him, are you?

Maid Marion I have to keep my promise.

Dime We're not going to work for the Sheriff any more. Let us smuggle you out of the castle, and away to Robin in the forest. We could do it.

Maid Marion Wish you could. (*looking at Babes*) I have no choice, you see.

Nickle Surely we can think of something.

Dime I know. Let's dig a tunnel.

Nickle What for?

Dime Well, that's what they always do, in the films. Then they climb down a rope made of sheets, and escape.

Nickle What are you talking about ? (*to Marion*) You don't think he's gone mad as well, do you?

Tom Perhaps it's catching.

Dime Alright then. I could bring you a cake with a file in it.

Nickle Dime...

Dime (*sadly*) I know. Dime, shut up.

Nickle Listen, there's someone coming.

Nurse (*entering*) Oh, is this the way to the wine cellar, I wonder? Isn't it dark? Oh, there you all are. Dear oh dear! Cheer up. I've been to parties like this before in (*local night spot*) Have a drink (*offers flask, which is refused*) No? Well I need one, to sober me up. (*takes a drink herself*)

Maid Marion Oh Nurse! I've got to marry the Sheriff.

Nurse I wouldn't if I were you. He's gone a bit, you know, one ball short of an over. He chased me round the castle saying he wished I was a deer. Well, I mean! A dear what?

Maid Marion I wish Robin was here.

Nurse That's it! I knew I'd come down here to tell you something. Robin is in the castle, and says he has some wonderful news.

Maid Marion What! Whatever can it be?

Nickle He's brave, coming to the castle. The Sheriff will have him for breakfast.

Dime No. He only eats straw, these days.

Maid Marion Come on Babes. Let's find out. The Sheriff said we were free anyway.

All exit, blackout

Scene 4

Grand Hall of the Castle of Nottingham. As for Act 1 Scene 1. As the curtains open, people are carrying things about, making preparations. Bunting is being put in place and other decorations for the finale. Sheriff, now himself again, is pleading with ladies from the chorus to marry him, as they move about across the stage. They all shake their heads and move off, saying 'No thank you' etc., He finally gets one of the kitchen maids to stop and listen to him

Sheriff Molly, er, it is Molly, isn't it?

Maid 1 My name's Joan.

Sheriff Of course. Now look Molly, er, Jenny, you know I've always liked you. Will you marry me? Don't say anything now, think about it. (*very short pause*) That's long enough. Well?

Maid 1 Oh! I don't think so.

Sheriff But, you <u>must</u> marry me. Someone's got to agree to marry me, quick.

Maid 1 Why? You're not in trouble, are you?

Sheriff What? Er, it's a long story. Well, will you, or not?

Maid 1 No. I've, got an understanding with one of the Merry Men, you see.

Sheriff Understanding! Is that what they call it these days!

Maid 1 Thanks for asking me though. Excuse me.

She makes to exit. On her way out she meets another maid

Maid 1 (*to Maid 2*) Here, guess what. Sheriff's just asked me to marry him!

Maid 2 Huh! Don't flatter yourself. He's asked everyone.

Maid 1 WHAT! Even you?

Maid 2 Do you mind! I was first! (*walks across stage and exits other side*)
Maid 1 WELL! (*she goes over to the Sheriff, pulls a face at him. and storms out*)
  HUH! I wouldn't marry you if there was nobody else left.
Sheriff Er, streuth. There is nobody else left. I've asked everyone else.

*Enter Nurse, humming to herself. She is busy dusting, or whatever, throughout
the next few lines, unaware of the Sheriff's presence until he speaks to her*

(*seeing Nurse*) Well, almost everyone else. No! I can't ask her. It's more than
flesh and blood can stand! Huh, what a punishment eh! I wish I'd been a good
Sheriff now. (*to audience*) Let this be a lesson to all you horrible kids. You'd
better change your ways or you could end up like me. (*he makes as though he
is about to go over to Nurse, then changes his mind*) Oh no, I won't ask her.
Audience Oh yes you will.
Sheriff I most definitely will not.
Audience You most definitely will.
Sheriff I most certainly, positively, absolutely, definitely will not, so there. I'd
  rather be a deer and eat straw.

To a tinkling of bells, enter Fairy Queen. Sheriff sees her and backs away

Not you again, Cloudy Spells! Haven't you done enough damage for one
pantomime? (*to audience*) She comes from Birkenhead, that's why they call
her the Ferry Queen! A Ferry Queen - without Mersey! Ha, ha! Well, laugh
you miserable lot. I'm flogging meself to death here!
Sunny Spells Your time is running out, Sheriff, I fear.
              Since you have failed, you must now become a deer.

Sunny Spells now prepares to carry out the spell

Sheriff No! Hang about! Not the Bumper Fun Book again, please! I didn't
  mean it. It's just my natural, bubbly sense of humour, you see. It gets the
  better of me, sometimes.
Sunny Spells You won't feel so brave in a minute, when you're running around
  on all fours. Now. (*prepares to cast spell again*)
Sheriff Streuth and double streuth! (*to audience*) Tell her to let me off. Go on.
Audience No!
Sheriff Tell her, go on.
Audience NO!

Sheriff I hope Santa gets stuck up your chimney! Alright, then, *(becoming mock heroic now, as some suitable, heroic, background, march music (**Music No 17**) comes up)* To do, or not to do? That is the question. There comes a time in a man's life, when he's gotta do, what he's gotta do. And it's a far, far better thing I do, and wish I didn't have to do. I'm telling you, it's true. Oh, what a to do! *(to Fairy Queen)* You're going to let me off at the last minute, aren't you? Just to show how kind and generous you are.

Sunny Spells No.

Sheriff You sure?

Sunny Spells Quite sure.

Background music fades

Sheriff Miserable old... I suppose I'll have to ask her then.

Sunny Spells This is your final chance, so do not fail.
                              Or suppers, from now on, are from a pail. *(exits)*

Sheriff I'll report her to the Society for the Prevention of Cruelty to Sheriffs. *(going to Nurse)* Here goes. Oh, there you are Nurse. Er, how nice to see you.

Nurse *(preoccupied)* Yes. You're back then. Someone must have paid the ransom.

Sheriff I was wondering. How do I stand for a small favour?

Nurse You don't stand, you kneel.

Sheriff Well, how about for a proposal then?

Nurse For a proposal you grovel.

Sheriff Now look here. I am the Sheriff, you know.

Nurse A very bad Sheriff.

Sheriff I'm reformed now. I'll give you the key to me heart, Nursie.

Nurse I'd sooner have the key to your wine cellar.

Sheriff Er, alright then, that as well.

Nurse Well, I don't know...

Sheriff You could do worse.

Nurse How?

Sheriff Well, er, you could, er, well, I don't know.

Nurse *(pointing down, indicating that he should kneel)* You won't hurt the Babes?

Sheriff *(sickly, and going down on one knee)* Er, alright then.

Nurse And you won't prevent Robin Hood and Marion getting married?

Sheriff Yes. I mean - no.

Nurse Ooh, I feel just like Elizabeth Taylor!

Sheriff Pity you don't look like her.

Nurse What?

Sheriff I said you look just like her.

Nurse You know just how to sweep a girl off her feet.

Sheriff And into the dustbin...

Nurse What?

Sheriff I said, I've just been - practising.

Nurse Oh. Now where shall we go for our honeymoon?

Sheriff Why don't you go to - er, Spain.

Nurse Is that where you want to go?

Sheriff No. I'll go somewhere else.

Nurse You must have your little joke! I forgive you, you little passion flower.

Song No 18

Song and dance number by Nurse Nightingale and the Sheriff. A comedy version of 'Get Me to the Church on Time' or 'People will say we're in Love' or 'The Flowers that Bloom in the Spring, Tra La'. If the former is chosen, the following verse is suggested, either on its own, or included with the original words

> I don't wanna turn into a reindeer.
> Being human's favourite every time.
> Fairy Queen's a rotter, but what you gotta do, you gotta.
> So, get me to the church on time.
> If I'm escaping, lock every door.
> If my mind I'm changing, pin me on the floor.
> Cos I've gotta do, what I am doing.
> And can't commit one teeny little crime.
> Babes come and kiss me, our quarrel now is history.
> If you get me to the church,
> Get me to the church,
> For gawd's sake get me to the church on time.

At the end of the song

Nurse Now, help me with the preparations, and be a dear...

Sheriff Don't ever call me 'deer' again.

Nurse Oh, alright dear...

Sheriff Er! Streuth.

Nurse Come along dear.

They both exit. Robin and Maid Marion enter from opposite sides of stage, and meet in the middle. The stage gradually empties

Robin Hood There you are Marion. I've been looking all over for you.

Maid Marion And I've been looking for you.

Robin Hood Isn't it wonderful? The Fairy Queen has sorted everything out.

Maid Marion Now we can get married at last.

Robin Hood Yes. And the Babes are safe too.

Maid Marion And get their true inheritance.

Robin Hood It's all really wonderful.

Maid Marion Everything's ready for the wedding. We had better get ready too.

Robin Hood Before the Sheriff changes his mind.

Maid Marion He won't do that, not with the Fairy Queen <u>and</u> Nurse keeping an eye on him. Everyone's been invited, and they'll be arriving soon. Come on.

They both exit, and the stage is left empty for a moment. Then, a dramatic chord, and the music for the finale begins

Song No 19

'On a Wonderful Day Like Today', or any up-tempo number from the show

Guests are arriving for wedding of Robin Hood to Maid Marion. Junior chorus; fairies, forest animals, toys, and village children etc., enter and take their bows. They are followed by the adult chorus. These all take up positions at the front, and sides of the stage, some may sit on the edge of the stage, leaving room for the principals to enter, and take their bows. The chorus should sing and clap to the music as the principals appear in the following order;

The Merry Men
Desmond
Fairy Queen and Firefly
Nickle and Dime
Sheriff and Nurse Nightingale
Tom and Mary

Maid Marion *and* **Robin Hood** *now enter. They have put on long cloaks over their costumes. They take their bows to loud cheers*

Final chorus *and* **curtain**

FURNITURE AND PROPERTY LIST

ACT 1

Scene 1

Personal: **Sheriff**, suitcases
Maid Marion, two letters
Fairy Queen, wand (required throughout)
Dime, rifle, club, outsize scissors, arrow, mallet, and
other weapons as available
Babes, bags or suitcases
Nurse, bottle or hip flask (required throughout)

Scene 3

On stage: Teacher's desk, blackboard, childrens' seats or desks,
dunce's hat, rope, dagger, hatchet, mallet
Personal: **Nurse**, cane, whistle, yellow card, red card
Children, paper balls to throw about

Scene 4

On stage: Bed, screen, collection of clothes etc., behind screen
Off stage: Community song words
Personal: **Nurse**, story book, large handkerchief

ACT 2

Scene 1

Personal: **Junior chorus**, Large leaves

Scene 2

On stage: Cooking pots etc., armoury and junk. Note on tree/board

Scene 3

Personal: **Nickle**, piece of paper

Scene 4

Personal;   **Chorus**, bunting etc.,
                Nurse, duster

LIGHTING PLOT

ACT 1

Scene 1

Scene 4

ACT 2

Scene 1

Scene 2

Scene 3

Scene 4

EFFECTS PLOT

General suggestions are given below. The amount, and complexity, of effects will depend on what the producer has at his disposal. For instance, a 'crash' may mean cymbals crashing, drums, or simply a chord on the piano etc., Remember, effects noises can often bring a pantomime to life, and their value should not be underestimated.

You may wish to have 'entry music' for some of the characters, Robin Hood or Sheriff, perhaps. This can be achieved by playing a properly orchestrated piece, or simply by playing a couple of chords on the piano.

ACT 1

Cue 6	As **Fairy Queen** enters	Page 13
	Tinkling bells, repeat as she exits	
Cue 7	**Sheriff**, 'I tell you it's the truth'	Page 20
	School bell rings	
Cue 8	**Nurse**, 'Sleep tight'	Page 23
	Stripper music number 9 slowly up.	
	Music down at, Nurse, 'You must be joking'	
Cue 9	As **Nurse** chases **Nickle** and **Dime**	Page 25
	Throughout chases, up to end page 28,	
	add suitable noises and crashes	

ACT 2

Cue 10	As **Fairy Queen** enters	Page 31
	Tinkling bells, repeat as she exits	
Cue 11	As **Nurse** falls to floor	Page 34
	Crash	
Cue 12	As **Fairy Queen** enters	Page 43
	Tinkling bells	
Cue 13	**Fairy Queen**, 'Beast you now shall be'	Page 44
	Flash	
Cue 14	As **Fairy Queen** exits	Page 47
	Tinkling bells	
Cue 15	As **Fairy Queen** enters	Page 50
	Tinkling bells	
Cue 16	**Sheriff**, 'Alright then'	Page 51
	March music number 17 slowly up.	
	Fade at, Fairy Queen, 'Quite sure'	

PRODUCTION NOTES

Scenery. Most of the scenery in this pantomime is fairly straightforward, and the script contains detailed notes. Obtaining small desks for the **Schoolroom Scene** may prove difficult, in which case benches, or even small chairs will do. The Sheriff's weapons, hammer, rope etc., will then need to be placed under one of the chairs at the back. The **Nursery Scene** chases should be organised around whatever exits and entrances are available. The more complicated, the better. Spooky music and bumps and crashes all add to the atmosphere.

Dances. There are three major dances for the juniors here. The Schoolroom dance, the Forest dance, and the Toys dance. If all these dances are being used, it is important to try to keep them as different as possible. You could use the same dancers, or vary your dance troupe here. Schoolroom scene; you may not have space on chairs, for all the junior dancers. If so, some will need to exit at the end of the dance.

Costumes. Fairy Queen will wear one costume. This should be a traditional Fairy Queen dress in white, pale cream, or pale blue, complete with sparkling wand and crown. **Firefly** will be a junior version of the Fairy Queen. For **Maid Marion** and **Robin Hood**, one costume will suffice. There is no time to change between their last exit and the finale walk down, so a cloak over the costume will be enough. Another option here might be to change after their previous exits (on pages 47 and 49) and to come on at page 52 already changed. Robin should wear the traditional 'forester' outfit of Lincoln Green. Short tunic, tights, soft boots, sword and boat-shaped hat with feather. The **Merry Men** will mostly wear Lincoln Green also. Friar Tuck should have a brown habit, and Will Scarlet may wear something red, to distinguish him from the rest. Much the Miller will be dressed as a 'country yokel' type, and rather dirty and dishevelled. A sprinkling of quivers, bows, bugles etc., here, will add to the effect. The **Sheriff, Nickle** and **Dime** will wear one costume of medieval pantomime type, except when they put on their disguise for the classroom scene. This may be a loosely fitting dress that drops over the costume below, and perhaps a bonnet. **Nurse** should have as many changes of costume as is possible. These should be as outrageous and as crazy as can be managed. There are opportunities for five elaborate, hilarious changes here, including night attire.

Desmond the Deer. If a deer costume proves difficult, it is a simple matter to change him to 'Harold the Horse'. He then becomes 'illtreated' by the Sheriff, and the rest of the script will stand the change, except that Nurse's "venison" joke will have to be cut. When Desmond changes to Sheriff, you will either have to do a quick change, putting the Sheriff in the front half of the deer, or you may have the Sheriff saying his lines from the wings, as the deer reacts on stage. If the latter, then some work will need to be done on timing, and voice levels, so that the deception is convincing.

I wish you great fun with this pantomime.

Jim Sperinck

Other **pantomimes** available from Jasper Publishing

By Jim Sperinck
RED RIDING HOOD
CINDERELLA
HUMPTY DUMPTY
ALADDIN
THE CANTERBURY TALES PANTO
DICK WHITTINGTON
ROBINSON CRUSOE
AN ARABIAN NIGHTS PANTO
MOTHER GOOSE

By Paul Alexander
ALADDIN
BABES IN THE WOOD
CINDERELLA
DICK WHITTINGTON
THREE POTTED PANTOS
MOTHER HUBBARD
PUSS IN BOOTS
OLD KING COLE
JACK AND THE BEANSTALK

By Richard Hills
ALADDIN
BABES IN THE WOOD
BEAUTY AND THE BEAST
GOODY TWO SHOES
RED RIDING HOOD
ROBINSON CRUSOE

By Michael Buchanan-Smart
OVER THE MOON
GOLDILOCKS AND THE THREE BEARS
HANSEL AND GRETEL
SPELLBOUND
ROBIN HOOD
RAPUNZEL

Plus many other plays, musicals etc.,
Please ask for our free catalogue

Jasper Publishing
1 Broad Street Hemel Hempstead Herts HP2 5BW
Tel: 01442 63461 Fax: 01442 217102